Grades **3-6**

Scott Foresman

Comprehension
Teacher's Guide and Student Worktext

Glenview, Illinois
Boston, Massachusetts
Chandler, Arizona
Upper Saddle River, New Jersey

D1502374

ISBN-13: 978-0-328-47835-4
ISBN-10:   0-328-47835-0
3 4 5 6 7 8 9 10 V084 18 17 16 15 14 13 12 11 10

Reading Street Intervention Kit

Program Overview

The *Reading Street Response to Intervention Kit* provides targeted instruction in core English-Language Arts standards for Grades 3 to 6 in each of the five critical areas of reading instruction: phonemic awareness, phonics and decoding, fluency, vocabulary, and comprehension. The Kit, designed for small-group or one-on-one instruction, includes lessons on core skills, allowing teachers to focus on the skills students need most and help them make rapid progress to achieve grade-level proficiency.

Each lesson includes three customized mini-lessons differentiated for the following reading and skill levels:

Mini-lesson 1: Level 1 (K to Grade 1)
Mini-lesson 2: Level 2 (Grades 2 to 3)
Mini-lesson 3: Level 3 (Grades 4 to 5)

For additional information about the *Reading Street Response to Intervention Kit*, see "How to Use This Kit" in the Placement Tests book on pp. T•4–T•6.

Comprehension Teacher's Guide and Student Worktext

The Teacher's Guide portion includes
- three-tiered, differentiated lessons for 15 core skills and strategies
- lessons on how to read nonfiction and fiction
- reinforcement for the strategies and routines used in the core program

The Student Worktext portion includes
- additional reading opportunities
- additional skills practice
- graphic organizers
- School+Home activities

Lesson Features

- **Set the scene** introduces the lesson topic to students.
- **Objectives** identify the instructional objectives for students.
- **Materials** list the Student Worktext components and additional supporting materials for the lesson, such as the Leveled Reader Database.
- **Direct teaching** is provided through explicit teacher modeling and consistent routines.
- **Model passages** allow teachers to model the skill or strategy.
- **Mini-lessons** allow for differentiated instruction.
- **Guided practice** for each mini-lesson consists of ample group practice with multiple response opportunities.
- **Independent practice (On Their Own)** allows students to read and apply skills independently or with teacher guidance.
- **If…/then…** provides teachers with specific activities for reinforcing skills.

Table of Contents
Comprehension

Comprehension
Teacher's Guide

How to Approach Fiction

Tell children that fiction tells a story about made-up characters and events. Story structure is the arrangement of a story from beginning to end. Explain that fiction always has characters, a setting, a plot, a theme, and a narrator.

Use the checklist below to explain to children that there are many strategies good readers use before, during, and after reading. For further instruction on teaching and applying these strategies, see the RTI Kit Implementation Guide.

BEFORE READING STRATEGIES

❏ **Activate Background Knowledge**   Background knowledge – information readers already know about a topic based on their reading and personal experience – allows children to make connections to people, places, and things from the real world.

❏ **Preview the text**   Previewing is a form of skimming and scanning the text before reading. Focus on features, such as text structure.

❏ **Predict and Set Purpose**   By predicting and setting a purpose for reading, struggling readers further connect themselves to text by personalizing their interaction with it.

DURING READING STRATEGIES

❏ **Question**   Explain to children that asking questions before, during, and after reading is an important tool for reading any type of text.

❏ **Monitor and Clarify Comprehension**   When monitoring their comprehension, children should determine not only *what* they don't understand, but also *why* they don't understand.

❏ **Draw Inferences**   Students can infer ideas about what the author is trying to present by identifying what they already know and combining what they know with text clues to come up with their own ideas.

❏ **Visualize**   Tell children that when they visualize, they collaborate with an author by taking the author's words and making them their own by creating pictures in their mind.

❏ **Code Text**   Coding text helps struggling readers monitor their comprehension and remember what they've read.

❏ **Use Graphic Organizers**   Completing graphic organizers while they read helps struggling readers organize, understand, and remember information both as they read and after reading.

AFTER READING STRATEGIES

❏ **Retell**   Remind struggling readers to include only main events and to think about the characters, the setting, and the plot as they retell.

❏ **Reflect**   To better understand the way they approach and navigate fiction, children should ask themselves questions, such as, "What features of the story's structure helped me understand the story?"

How to Approach Expository Text

Tell children that expository text tells about real people, places, or things. Expository text can be organized in many different ways, such as by cause and effect, problem and solution, question and answer, comparison and contrast, description, and sequence. Use the checklist below to explain the strategies good readers use before, during, and after reading. For further instruction on teaching and applying these strategies, see the RTI Kit Implementation Guide.

BEFORE READING STRATEGIES

❏ **Activate Prior Knowledge**   Background knowledge allows students to connect to the text.

❏ **Build Background Knowledge**   To build background knowledge, readers can stop and explain a text-to-self connection that arises in their thinking.

❏ **Set a Purpose for Reading**   Keep struggling readers focused and motivated by clearly establishing a purpose.

❏ **Overview the Text**   Focus overviewing, a form of skimming and scanning the text before reading, on features such as text structure.

DURING READING STRATEGIES

❏ **Question**   Asking questions before, during, and after reading helps readers evaluate their understanding.

❏ **Determine Important Ideas**   To identify important ideas, students can refer to the expository features and structures, such as headings.

❏ **Monitor and Clarify Comprehension**   Use background knowledge and strategies such as asking questions to clarify understanding.

❏ **Draw Inferences**   Students can infer ideas about what the author is trying to present by combining what they already know with text clues.

❏ **Synthesize Information**   Readers can reach new insights that change the way they think by reviewing, sorting, and sifting information.

❏ **Visualize**   When struggling readers get pictures in their mind while reading, they are more likely to keep reading.

❏ **Code Text**   Coding text helps struggling readers monitor their comprehension and remember what they've read.

❏ **Highlight**   Highlighting important ideas in text is a valuable strategy.

❏ **Use Graphic Organizers**   Visual displays of key ideas help struggling readers categorize content and pull important ideas from text.

❏ **Understand New Vocabulary**   Reading on, rereading, and reading surrounding sentences helps determine the meaning of new words.

AFTER READING STRATEGIES

❏ **Summarize**   Tell struggling readers to include only main ideas they summarize.

❏ **Reflect**   Children should ask themselves questions, such as, "What features helped me understand the text?"

Author's Purpose

Objectives:

- Identify and distinguish common reasons for writing, including to persuade, inform, express, and entertain.
- Adjust reading depending on author's purpose(s).
- Recognize that authors usually have more than one purpose for writing.

MATERIALS

Worktext pp. 2–7
Four-Column Chart, p. 95
T-Chart, p. 101
Three-Column Chart, p. 102
Leveled Reader Database

Set the scene Explain that authors usually have more than one purpose for writing. Common purposes include writing to persuade, to inform, to express, and to entertain.

Model and teach Read aloud "Disappearing Tuna."

Disappearing Tuna

Tuna has been a main part of many Asian diets for years. Today people around the world have started eating tuna as well. Fishing companies are working more to meet the demand. The fish in the oceans are caught faster than they can reproduce. Scientists estimate that the number of tuna has dropped over 70% in the past 30 years because of overfishing. Yet fishing companies in many parts of the world are not changing how they fish. The world community needs to set limits on fishing tuna. If not, this fish may soon die out.

Display a Four-Column Chart from Worktext p. 95 with *Inform, Entertain, Persuade,* and *Express* as column headings. Give the following explanation for each and write it in the appropriate column. When authors write to *inform,* they give the reader important information. Authors write to *entertain* when they want to tell an interesting story. When authors write to *persuade,* they try to make the reader think or act a certain way. When they write to *express,* they describe something to create a mood or feeling.

In "Disappearing Tuna," the author gives information, such as facts about the decrease in tuna. The author also tries to convince the reader that there should be limits on fishing. The main purposes are to inform and to persuade.

Mini-Lesson 1

Remind students that...

- authors write to *inform* to give the reader important information.
- authors write to *entertain* when they want to tell an interesting story.
- authors write to *persuade* when they want to make the reader think or act a certain way.
- when authors write to *express,* they describe something to create a mood or feeling.

Guide Practice

Read the story aloud.

Opening Night

It was my chance to shine. It was opening night, and I had a solo. I had practiced for months. My whole family was there to watch me.

The curtain opened. There was not a sound. My shoes tapped on the wood floor as I took my place. My mouth was dry. My hands were wet.

I opened my mouth to sing the first note. Just then, I heard a loud whistle. My heart dropped. I knew it was my brother. But I could not stop now. I took a deep breath and started singing.

- What is the story about? *(someone singing at a show)*
- How did the story make you feel? *(nervous for the singer)* Help students point out specific details.
- Why do you think the author wrote this? *(to entertain, to express)*
- How can you tell? *(gives details that help the reader know the narrator's feelings)*

If... students have trouble identifying the author's purposes,

then... work through the process of elimination with all four purposes.

On Their Own As students read "Mysterious Cicadas" on Worktext p. 2 independently or with you, have them use the T-Chart on p. 101. For additional practice, assign p. 3.

Mini-Lesson 2

Remind students that...
- authors usually have more than one purpose for writing.
- they can figure out an author's purpose by looking at details in the text and the words the author uses.

Guide Practice
Tell students that authors don't always tell their purpose for writing. The reader often has to figure it out. Reread "Disappearing Tuna" aloud on the previous page. Ask:
- What is the text about? *(overfishing tuna)*
- What details help you figure out that the author wants to inform readers? *(The text gives information, such as facts about the history of tuna fishing.)*
- Think about the words the author uses. How do they help you figure out that one of the author's purposes is to persuade? *(The statement "The world community needs to set limits" urges the reader to think and act to change tuna fishing.)*

If... students have trouble understanding that the text is likely *not* intended to entertain or to express,
then... explain how the article to might change if those *were* the author's purposes, such as including a particular fisherman's story.

On Their Own As students read "Mountain Lions Back in the Midwest?" on Worktext p. 4 independently or with you, have them use the Four-Column Chart on p. 95 with the four author's purposes listed as they read. For additional practice, assign p. 5.

Mini-Lesson 3

Remind students that...
- authors usually have more than one purpose for writing.
- they can figure out an author's purpose by looking at details in the text and the words the author uses.
- they should adjust their reading depending on the author's purposes.
- they can make and support judgments of the author's purpose(s).

Guide Practice
Explain that knowing the author's purposes can help readers adjust how they read the text. For example, if the author's purpose is to inform, students might read slowly, rereading facts and studying any graphics for better understanding.

Reread "Disappearing Tuna" aloud. Ask:
- What do you think are the author's purposes for writing the article? *(to inform and to persuade)*

- How does identifying the author's purposes help you know how to read the text? *(Students will likely read the text slowly to check that they understand the information.)*
- How convincing is the article? How would you make the article more convincing? *(Students may feel the article is persuasive because it offers facts and statistics as support. They may want additional facts.)*

If... students have difficulty supporting their judgments about the author's success in meeting his or her purpose,
then... have them look for specific features in the text that support their view.

On Their Own As students read "Neighbors" on Worktext p. 6 independently or with you, have them use the Three-Column Chart on p. 102 to determine the author's purpose, whether it was successful, and why. For additional practice, assign p. 7.

Comprehension Lesson 2
Cause and Effect

Objectives:
- Identify causes and effects.
- Recognize cause-effect clue words.
- Identify implied causes in text.
- Recognize cause-effect as a form of nonfiction text structure.

MATERIALS
Worktext pp. 8–13
Cause and Effect Organizer, p. 92
Leveled Reader Database

Set the scene Explain that a *cause* is why something happened, and an *effect* is what happened. We can identify an effect by asking "What happened?" and identify a cause by asking "Why did this happen?" Look for clue words such as *so* and *because*.

Model and teach Read the article aloud.

The Nile and Ancient Egypt

Most of Egypt is desert. Yet the land around the Nile River is full of life. <u>Because</u> it was located near the Nile, Ancient Egypt became successful.

Farming was possible <u>because</u> the river flowed through Egypt. Each spring, heavy rains and melting snow poured into the river, <u>so</u> water from the Nile flooded the land around the river. When the water levels sank in the fall, the river left behind dark, rich soil. People planted crops in the rich soil.

The river was also important to Ancient Egypt for other food and supplies, as well as for travel and protection. People used plants that grew near the river to make ropes, clothing, and paper. The river's shape and its waterfalls also made it hard for people to travel into Egypt. <u>Therefore</u>, the river protected Egypt from enemies. Inside the country, the river connected the people of Egypt.

Display a Cause and Effect Organizer from p. 92. I'll read again to look for clue words. *Because* is a clue word. I ask myself, "What happened?" This sentence says that Ancient Egypt became successful. "Why did this happen?" Egypt was near the Nile. **Continue modeling.**

 **Mini-Lesson 1**

Remind students that…
- an effect is what happens, and a cause is why that thing happens.
- clue words are sometimes present in cause-effect relationships.
- one effect may have more than one cause.

Guide Practice
Ask students to find the cause-and-effect relationships in the following sentences:
- *It had been raining all month, so farmers did not plant crops yet.* What happened? *(Farmers did not plant crops yet.)* Why did this happen? *(It had been raining all month.)*
- *Marco lost his wallet Saturday. He couldn't buy his sister a birthday gift like he had planned.* What happened? *(Marco couldn't buy his sister a birthday gift.)* Why did this happen? *(Marco lost his wallet.)*
- *The Braves lost the game because their pitcher was injured and two of their best players were out sick.* What happened? *(The Braves lost the game.)* Why did this happen? *(Their pitcher was injured, and two of their best players were out sick.)*

If… students have trouble identifying cause and effect, **then…** help them first identify clue words.

 On Their Own As students read "A New Life" on Worktext p. 8 independently or with you, have them complete a Cause and Effect Organizer from p. 92 to identify causes and effects. For additional practice, assign p. 9.

Mini-Lesson 2

Remind students that...

- an effect is what happens, and a cause is why that thing happens.
- one effect may have several causes, and one cause may have several effects.
- causes are not always directly stated in the text.

Guide Practice

Review that a cause can have multiple effects, and an effect can have multiple causes. Reread the second paragraph of "The Nile and Ancient Egypt" aloud. What two things caused the Nile to flood? *(melting snow and heavy rains)* What clue word signals that the flooding was an effect? *(so)*

Explain that causes might not always be directly stated. You can figure out a cause by asking, "Why might this have happened?" Reread the last paragraph of "The Nile and Ancient Egypt" aloud. The first sentence says that the river was important to Ancient Egypt for travel. Why might river travel have been important to the success of Ancient Egypt? *(Possible answers: River travel helped people buy and sell things throughout Egypt; it allowed people to expand their society; it was a faster and easier way to travel than the desert.)*

If... students have trouble identifying valid causes that are not stated directly,
then... have them check that they can support their answers with the text and prior knowledge.

On Their Own Have students read "Changes" on Worktext p. 10 independently or with you, filling out the Cause and Effect Organizer from p. 92. For additional practice, assign p. 11.

Mini-Lesson 3

Remind students that...

- cause-effect relationships can be signaled with clue words and phrases, such as *therefore, as a result,* and *consequently.*
- clue words are not always present in cause-effect relationships.
- a paragraph or text can be organized by cause-effect text structure.

Guide Practice

Review and expand instruction of cause-effect clue words. Clue words that signal a cause include *because, reason,* and *since.* Clue words that signal an effect include *so, consequently, as a result,* and *therefore.* Reread the last paragraph of "The Nile and Ancient Egypt." The paragraph says that the Nile's shape and waterfalls made it hard for people to enter Egypt. Is the fact that Egypt was protected from enemies a cause or an effect of the river's shape and waterfalls? *(effect)* How do you know? *(The clue word* therefore *signals effect.)*

Reread "The Nile and Ancient Egypt" aloud. Explain that the text is organized by cause-effect structure. Point out the sentence, "Because it was near the Nile, Ancient Egypt became successful." Each of the following paragraphs in the text gives reasons (causes) why the Nile made Ancient Egypt successful. One cause is that the Nile made farming possible. What are other causes? *(The Nile provided food, supplies, travel routes, and protection.)*

If... students have trouble recognizing cause-effect text structure,
then... have them first identify the author's main point and determine the causes or effects related to that point.

On Their Own Have students read "A Birthday Surprise" on Worktext p. 12 independently or with you, using the Cause and Effect Organizer from p. 92. For additional practice, assign p. 13.

Comprehension Lesson 3
Compare and Contrast

Objectives:

- Recognize comparison-contrast relationships.
- Recognize clue words that signal comparison-contrast relationships.
- Compare and contrast between what one reads and what one already knows.
- Compare and contrast within and across texts.

MATERIALS

Worktext pp. 14–19
T-Chart, p. 101
Leveled Reader Database

Set the scene Point out that when students compare, they tell how two or more things are alike. When they contrast, they tell how things are different. Clue words, such as *like, unlike,* and *but,* show how things are alike or different. You can compare and contrast things within a text or with the text and your own life. You can also compare and contrast different texts.

Model and teach Read aloud "Rob's New Shoes."

Rob's New Shoes

Rob rushed home from school. Today he made the basketball team! Rob was unlike most of the other players on the team. He was much taller than everyone else. Other players were faster, but Rob had bigger feet and hands. No one could steal the ball from him. Like the best players, Rob could easily make baskets.

Rob stopped his mother and told her the news. She was excited at first. Then Rob told her he needed new shoes for practice. "Hmm," said Rob's mother. Rob's feet were already bigger than those of his father, and Rob was only 12. That night, they bought a pair of basketball shoes. Rob couldn't wait to try them out.

Help students use the T-Chart from p. 101 to compare and contrast things in the story. One thing I can compare and contrast is how Rob is like and unlike other players. Write *Rob* and *Other Players* as the column heads. I can compare and contrast physical traits, basketball skills, and shoes. Model filling in the chart.

Mini-Lesson 1

Remind students that...

- comparisons tell how things are alike, and contrasts tell how things are different.
- they can make comparisons and contrasts themselves.

Guide Practice

Reread "Rob's New Shoes," and ask students the following questions:

- What does this story remind you of in your own life? *(Students, their friends, or their siblings may be in sports, may be going through growth spurts, or may have parents with similar reactions as that of Rob's mom.)*
- How is Rob like or unlike other kids you know? *(Students may have friends or siblings who are also tall and good at sports; by contrast, Rob may seem much bigger than them or other kids they know.)*

- How is Rob like most basketball players? How is he unlike most basketball players? *(Rob is good at basketball, but he is slower and physically larger than most players.)*

Then have students list how Rob is like and unlike each of his parents.

If... students have trouble identifying likenesses and differences,

then... reread the paragraph and ask specific questions, such as, "How are Rob's feet like or unlike his father's feet?"

On Their Own As students read "Blue and Eddie" on Worktext p. 14 independently or with you, have them complete the T-Chart from p. 101. For additional practice, assign p. 15.

Mini-Lesson 2

Remind students that…
- comparisons tell how two or more things are alike, and contrasts tell how two or more things are different.
- clue words, such as *like, unlike,* and *but* can show comparison and contrast.

Guide Practice
Help students understand clue words that signal compare and contrast. Words such as *like* and *both* signal comparison, and *unlike* and *but* signal contrast.

Reread the first paragraph from "Rob's New Shoes" aloud.
- Reread the third sentence. What is the compare or contrast clue word? *(unlike)* What does it tell you? *(Rob is different from the other players on his team.)*
- Reread the fifth sentence. What is the compare or contrast clue word? *(but)* What does it tell you about how Rob is like or unlike the other players? *(It shows*

that Rob is different from them because he isn't as fast, and he has bigger hands and feet.)
- Reread the last sentence. What clue word do you see? *(like)* What is compared or contrasted? *(Rob's skill at making baskets is compared to the best players' skill at making baskets.)*

If… students have trouble identifying comparisons and contrasts,
then… focus on identifying clue words first.

On Their Own As students read "Summer Camp" on Worktext p. 16 independently or with you, have them complete a T-Chart from p. 101 to compare and contrast. For additional practice, assign p. 17.

Mini-Lesson 3

Remind students that…
- comparisons tell how two or more things are alike, and contrasts tell how two or more things are different.
- comparisons and contrasts are often not signaled by clue words.
- they can compare and contrast within and across texts.

Guide Practice
Reread "Rob's New Shoes" on the previous page. Then read aloud the paragraph below.

Tryouts

When she was 12, Julie tried out for volleyball. She was not as tall or as big as most of the other players. Yet Julie was strong. When she served, few players could return the ball. She was also good at setting. The day after tryouts, the coach posted the players' names. Julie spotted her name. She had made the team!

- How is Julie unlike other players on the volleyball team? *(She is not as tall or big as them.)*
- How is Julie like Rob in "Rob's New Shoes"? *(They are both 12, trying out for a sport, unlike their other teammates, and both make the team.)*
- How are Julie and Rob different? *(They try out for different sports; Julie is short, but Rob is tall; and Rob buys shoes, but Julie doesn't.)*

If… students have trouble comparing and contrasting across texts,
then… ask specific questions, such as "How are Julie and Rob physically different?"

On Their Own As students read "Ye Xian" and "Cinderella" on Worktext p. 18 independently or with you, have them complete a Four-Column Chart from p. 95 to compare and contrast. For additional practice, assign p. 19.

Comprehension Lesson 4
Main Idea and Details

Objectives:
- Identify a stated main idea.
- Identify supporting details.
- Identify an implied main idea.

MATERIALS
Worktext pp. 20–25
Main Idea Organizer, p. 96
Leveled Reader Database

Set the scene Explain that the main idea tells what the passage is mostly about and that details are pieces of information that tell about the main idea. Readers identify the main idea and supporting details to understand what they read.

Model and teach Read aloud "The Beginning of Basketball."

The Beginning of Basketball

On a winter day in 1891, snow and ice covered the playground at a school. The schoolboys were bored and needed to work off their extra energy. A teacher took two baskets and nailed them to the wall on each end of the room. Then he took a soccer ball and aimed it at one of the baskets. He wanted to get the ball into the basket, but it was hard to do. Soon everyone wanted to try. They took turns.

At last someone threw the ball into the basket. Everyone cheered. Then the boys wondered how they could get the ball out of the basket. No one could reach that high. The teacher got a ladder and got the ball out. This was how the first game of basketball was played.

Model how to determine the main idea. First, ask, "What is the passage about?" I think it's about *basketball*. All of the sentences tell about basketball. Then I ask, "What is the most important idea about this topic?" The title and sentences describe the first game of basketball. I think the main idea is *how basketball started*. Write this in the Main Idea Organizer on p. 96. Finally, I ask, "What are some details that tell more about the main idea?" Continue modeling.

Remind students that...
- the main idea is what the text is mostly about.
- the main idea is the most important idea of a text.
- details tell more about the main idea.

Guide Practice
Read aloud "Our Farm."

Our Farm
We live on a farm. We have a few sheep, some cows, some chickens, and a horse. I help find the eggs. My brother milks the cows. My dad feeds all of the animals. Sometimes we ride our horse. I like living on a farm.

Display a Main Idea Organizer from p. 96. The main idea is what the selection is all about. What is "Our Farm" all about? *(living on a farm)* Write that in the organizer. How do you know this is the main idea?

(Every sentence tells about farm life.) Details are small pieces of information that tell more about the main idea. What are some details? *(The family has sheep, cows, chickens, and a horse; the narrator helps find eggs, and so on.)* Add these to the organizer.

If... students have trouble identifying the main idea, **then...** have them look at the first three sentences and ask, "What are all these sentences about?"

On Their Own As students read "How I Make My Lunch" on Worktext p. 20 independently or with you, have them complete a Main Idea Organizer. For additional practice, assign p. 21.

Mini-Lesson 2

Remind students that...

• the main idea is the most important idea about the topic.

• the main idea is not always stated directly in the passage.

• supporting details tell more about the main idea.

Guide Practice
Read the paragraph aloud.

You probably know that robins like to eat earthworms. That is not the only thing robins eat. They also eat beetles and caterpillars. Yet robins mostly eat fruit and berries.

The topic is what the passage is about in a word or two. What is the topic? *(robins)* What is the most important idea about this topic, or the main idea? Some main ideas are not in the text, so readers must use details to figure them out. *(Robins eat different things.)* Write this in the organizer on p. 96. How do you know this is the main idea? *(Each sentence tells about things robins eat.)*

To find supporting details, look for sentences that give more information about the main idea. One supporting detail is that robins like to eat earthworms. What are some other supporting details? *(Robins eat beetles and caterpillars.)*

If... students have trouble identifying an implied main idea,

then... have them first think about what the supporting details are all about.

 On Their Own As students read "All About Bears" on Worktext p. 22 independently or with you, have them complete a Main Idea Organizer. For additional practice, assign p. 23.

Mini-Lesson 3

Remind students that...

• the main idea is the most important idea about the topic.

• a main idea may or may not be stated in the text.

• they can determine the main idea of a paragraph, passage, or article.

• supporting details describe or explain the main idea.

Guide Practice
Read the article aloud.

César Chávez
When César Chávez was a child, his family had to move often in search of work. They worked long days in fields under the sun. His family was not alone. Many other families also moved often and worked hard in the fields.

Life was hard for the Chávez family and other workers. They earned little money working on other people's farms.

When Chávez grew up, he decided it was time for things to change. In 1962 he started a group for migrant workers. The group spoke about the problems of working in the fields. People listened. They made changes to help the workers.

What are most of the sentences in "César Chávez" about? *(Chávez worked to improve the lives of migrant workers.)* That is the main idea. What is one supporting detail? *(In 1962, Chávez started a group for migrant workers.)*

If... students have trouble correctly identifying the main idea,

then... have them check that they can justify their main idea with supporting details.

 On Their Own As students read "Destination Hawaii" on Worktext p. 24 independently or with you, have them complete a Main Idea Organizer from p. 96.

Comprehension Lesson 5
Sequence

Objectives:
- Identify sequence of events.
- Identify sequence clue words.
- Recognize simultaneous events and events told out of sequence.
- Organize events in sequence order.

MATERIALS

Worktext pp. 26–31
Story Sequence B Organizer, p. 100
Time Line, p. 103
Leveled Reader Database

Set the scene Explain that when you tell the sequence, or order, of events in a selection, you tell what happens first, next, and last. Selections may have clue words, such as *first, next,* and *then,* or they may include dates or times, such as *1982* or *the next morning.* Identify the sequence of events as you read to better understand the selection.

Model and teach Read aloud "The Fox."

The Fox

Carlos's family likes to be outside, so they decided to go on a camping trip. The family drove to the campsite and spent the day hiking.

Carlos wanted to see a fox, but he did not see one all day. He was very disappointed. That night, after the family had eaten dinner and cleaned up, they went to bed. But Carlos forgot to put the salad away. He left it on the picnic table.

The next morning, Carlos woke up before anyone else. Then he came out of the tent, and he heard a funny little noise. A young fox had its nose inside the bag of salad that Carlos had left out the night before. Finally, Carlos had seen a fox!

Fill out the Story Sequence B Organizer from p. 100 with students. To help me understand the story, I look for the order in which things happen. I'm going to read the story again and picture what happens in my mind. **Read the first sentence. What happens?** *(Carlos's family goes camping.)* Write this in the organizer.

Next, I think about the next thing that happens. I remember that the family drove to the campsite and spent the day hiking. I write that in the *Next* box. **Continue modeling.**

Remind students that...
- in a story, something happens first, next, and last.
- sequence is the order in which things happen.

Guide Practice

Help students understand sequence by giving them everyday examples. Then ask them to help you find the sequence in other sentences.
- *First, Luis went to the store. Then he looked at the fruits and vegetables. Last, Luis bought apples, oranges, and a tomato.* What happens first? *(Luis went to the store.)* What happens next? *(He looked at the fruit and vegetables.)* What happens last? *(He bought apples, oranges, and a tomato.)*

Repeat the procedure with these sentences.
- *Jamal walked home from school. He fed his dog, and then he took him for a walk.*

- *First, Lisa went to the library to study. Then she had her sister quiz her. At last, Lisa took her test.*

If... students have trouble identifying the sequence of events,

then... act out a basic process with a clear sequence, such as sharpening a broken pencil.

On Their Own As students read "In the Leaves" on Worktext p. 26 independently or with you, have them complete a Story Sequence B Organizer from p. 100. For additional practice, assign p. 27.

Mini-Lesson 2

Remind students that...
- sequence is the order of events.
- words such as *first, next,* and *then* are sequence clue words.
- dates and times can act as sequence clue words.

Guide Practice

Explain that clue words, such as *first, next,* and *then,* as well as dates and times, can help readers identify sequence. Also remind students that clue words are not always in the text. Read aloud the paragraph below.

On Monday, Paul had a guitar lesson. He went home and practiced. Then he practiced with his friend Mike on Wednesday and Thursday. On Friday night, Paul and Mike decided to start their own band.

What clue words are there? *(Monday, then, Wednesday, Thursday,* and *Friday)* What happens first? *(Paul had his guitar lesson.)* How do you know it happened first? *(the clue word* Monday; *the event happens before the others)* Complete a Time Line from p. 103 together for the other events.

If... students have trouble identifying the second event, **then...** explain that not all events in a sequence have clue words, but students can picture them in their mind to figure out the sequence.

 On Their Own As students read "Flash's First Race" on Worktext p. 28 independently or with you, have them complete a Time Line. For additional practice, assign p. 29.

Mini-Lesson 3

Remind students that...
- sequence is the order of events.
- some events happen at the same time.
- sometimes texts tell events out of order.

Guide Practice

Point out that some events happen simultaneously, or at the same time. *Meanwhile, while,* and *during* are clue words for events that happen at the same time. Some selections tell events out of order. Read aloud "Raccoons!"

Raccoons!

Last night Sara watched a movie on TV. During the movie, she heard loud crashing outside. Sara went to look. Then she saw that the garbage cans were tipped over, and garbage was everywhere. Next, Sara saw two raccoons staring at her. Yesterday, Sara had taken out the garbage. She must have forgotten to close the lids tightly.

Which events happen simultaneously? *(Sara was watching a movie, and she heard crashing.)* What event is told out of order? *(Sara had taken out the garbage yesterday.)* Complete a Time Line from p. 103 with students showing the events in sequence order.

If... students have trouble identifying correct sequence, **then...** help them check that their sequence makes sense.

 On Their Own As students read "How Crayons Are Made" on Worktext p. 30 independently or with you, have them complete a Time Line. For additional practice, assign p. 31.

Comprehension Lesson 6
Draw Conclusions

Objectives:
- Draw conclusions, or figure out more about, characters and events in a story or article.
- Use what you already know to help draw conclusions.
- Use evidence from the text to help draw conclusions.
- Check that conclusions are logical and valid.

MATERIALS
Worktext pp. 32–37
Three-Column Chart, p. 102
Leveled Reader Database

Set the scene Explain that drawing conclusions means to think about facts and details and decide something about them. Readers put together what they read with what they know about real life to draw conclusions and understand what they read.

Model and teach Read aloud "At the Ocean."

At the Ocean

Kim and her family went to the ocean for the day. In the car, Kim's father had said, "I don't know, kids. It kind of looks like it's going to rain." He grumbled that the sky looked dark and cloudy. Kim's mother frowned. She was hoping for perfect weather.

At the beach, Kim's brother Ben grabbed his surfboard and ran into the waves. Behind him, Kim walked slowly into the cold water, careful not to get splashed. Kim's mother picked up Kim's little brother Johnny and carried him to the shore to get his feet wet. Johnny kicked his feet. He laughed at the waves. Meanwhile, Kim's father sat alone under the umbrella and read his paper. Kim noticed her father was right. It was starting to sprinkle.

Display a Three-Column Chart from p. 102 with the headings *What I Read, What I Know,* and *My Conclusions.* What conclusion can you draw about how each character feels about the beach? First, how does Kim's father feel? In the story, he grumbles about the weather. I know that when people go to the beach, they usually go swimming or lie in the sun. I conclude that Kim's father does not like the beach today because of the weather. **Continue modeling.**

Mini-Lesson 1

Remind students that...
- they draw conclusions in real life all the time.
- drawing conclusions about a text means putting together what you know and what you read to figure something out.

Guide Practice
Remind students they often draw conclusions in real life. For example, if your friend goes camping and comes back with itchy red bumps, you can determine that your friend was bitten by mosquitoes.

Ask students to put together what they know with what they hear from the sentences to figure out what happened.
- *My sister saw a pretty rose. She put her hand around the stem to pick it. Then she yelled, "Ow!"* What happened? *(The sister was pricked by a thorn on the rose.)*

- *Keisha's mom usually drives her to school. Today her dad drove her. Keisha said she hoped her mom felt better soon.* What happened? *(Keisha's mom stayed home because she was sick.)*

If... students have trouble understanding the concept of drawing conclusions,
then... remind them that, in this context, *draw* means "to figure out," not "to create a picture."

On Their Own As students read "Spring Tryouts" on Worktext p. 32 independently or with you, have them complete a Three-Column Chart from p. 102. For additional practice, assign p. 33.

Remind students that...

- drawing conclusions about a text means putting together what you know and what you read to figure something out.
- they can reread a text to check that their conclusions make sense.

Guide Practice

Reread "At the Ocean" on the previous page. Remind students about the conclusion you drew about Kim's father. Then ask: About how old do you think Johnny is? Have students look at the text for clues. Then have them use what they know to draw a conclusion. *(The text says Johnny is Kim's little brother. Kim's mom carries him, and Johnny laughs and kicks his feet. Johnny is being carried, and he acts the way babies do in the water. I think he must be a baby.)*

Then have students draw conclusions to answer the questions.

- How does Kim's mother feel about Kim's father's comments about the weather? *(She's unhappy because she want it to be a nice day.)*
- How does Kim feel about the ocean water? *(She thinks it is cold.)*

If... students have trouble drawing correct conclusions, **then...** display the story and circle details in the text that help students answer the questions.

 On Their Own As students read "Late Again" on Worktext p. 34 independently or with you, have them complete a Three-Column Chart from p. 102. For additional practice, assign p. 35.

Remind students that...

- drawing conclusions means putting together what you know and what you read or see to figure something out.
- they can support and verify their conclusions with facts and details from the text.
- they can check that conclusions are logical and valid.

Guide Practice

Point out that as students read, they can draw conclusions to figure out more about the text. When you draw conclusions, ask, "How can I support this conclusion with details from the text?" and "How does it make sense based on what I know about real life?" Encourage students to check that authors' conclusions also seem logical.

Explain why some conclusions are *not* valid. Reread "At the Ocean." Ask: Why is the conclusion that Kim does not

like the water not valid? *(The text says Kim walked slowly into the cold water, careful not to get splashed. Though she does not run like Ben, there is no support that she does not like the water. She may walk slowly because the water is cold.)*

If... students have trouble determining whether a conclusion is valid, **then...** have them check if it is supported both by the text and by common sense.

 On Their Own As students read "Town Shocked by Walking Catfish" on Worktext p. 36 independently or with you, have them complete a Three-Column Chart from p. 102. For additional practice, assign p. 37.

Comprehension Lesson 7
Character

Objectives:
- Identify characters and character traits.
- Infer character traits and predict characters' future actions.
- Recognize character motivation.
- Determine traits based on character interaction and how a character changes.

MATERIALS

Worktext pp. 38–43
Four-Column Chart, p. 95
Leveled Reader Database

Set the scene Explain that characters are the people and animals in a story. Students can identify what characters look like, say, think, feel, and do. They can figure out why characters act the way they do and how they change.

Model and teach Read aloud "Rush."

Rush

The bell rang. Carmen pulled her long, red hair into a knot. She slammed her books in her locker and ran home. She was practicing for track.

Carmen saw her mom driving, and she sprinted up the driveway. "I beat you!" Her mom sighed. "Hurry up and change. We're going to see Grandfather." Carmen wiped her forehead. "Do I have to go?"

"Right now," said her mother, eyeing Carmen's torn jeans and sneakers. "And put on a nice dress." Carmen frowned. Her grandfather's was the last place she wanted to go. It was boring there, and the Home smelled funny.

Then Carmen remembered her last visit. Someone had yelled at her for running in the hallway. "Hey, that girl is going to be in the Olympics someday!" Grandfather shot back. Everyone thought Carmen's running was childish, but Grandfather told her to join track. Maybe it would be good to visit him again.

Display a Four-Column Chart from Worktext p. 95. Label the columns *Looks Like, Does, Says,* and *Thinks or Feels.* Fill in the chart with students.

Remind students that...
- people and animals in a story are characters.
- characters can be real or make-believe.
- as they read, they can identify what characters say, do, and feel.

Guide Practice

Reread "Rush" aloud. Who are the characters? *(Carmen, Carmen's mother, and Carmen's grandfather)* Are the characters realistic or make-believe? *(realistic)* How can you tell? *(Their traits are like those of real-life people.)*

Then have students identify what the characters say, do, and feel.
- How does Carmen get home from school? *(She runs.)* What does this tell you about her? *(She is competitive and likes to run.)*
- How does Carmen feel about seeing her grandfather? *(She does not want to go at first, but then she does.)*

What actions, words, or thoughts help you decide this? *(Carmen first asks, "Do I have to?" about seeing him. She thinks the Home is boring. Then she remembers that Grandfather supported her running.)*

If... students have trouble identifying the characters' feelings in a story,
then... point out examples of characters telling how they feel.

On Their Own As students read "The Watch" on Worktext p. 38 independently or with you, have them complete a Four-Column Chart on p. 95. For additional practice, assign p. 39.

Mini-Lesson 2

Remind students that...

- they can describe a character's physical appearance; what the character says, thinks, and feels; and what he or she does.
- they can infer character traits through characters' words and actions.

Guide Practice

Reread "Rush" on the previous page. Point out that sometimes authors do not tell everything about their characters. Then readers need to use clues in the story to learn about them.

- What does Carmen's mother do when Carmen races her to the house and says, "I beat you"? *(She sighs and tells her to change clothes.)* Based on what Carmen's mother says and does, how do you think she feels about Carmen's running? *(She doesn't seem to take it seriously.)*

- What does Carmen do when her mother asks her to put on a dress? *(She frowns.)* Based on Carmen's reaction, how do you think she feels about dressing up? *(She doesn't like it.)*

If... students have trouble identifying the characters' thoughts or feelings in a story when they are not explicitly stated,

then... point out examples of characters showing feelings through action and dialogue.

On Their Own As students read "Mr. Field's Dogs" on Worktext p. 40 independently or with you, have them complete a Four-Column Chart on p. 95. For additional practice, assign p. 41.

Mini-Lesson 3

Remind students that...

- they can describe characters by identifying their traits.
- they can determine character traits based on how other characters act toward a character and what they say about him or her.
- they can determine if, how, and why a character changes during a story.

Guide Practice

Reread "Rush" on the previous page. Explain that readers can learn about a character through other characters' actions and dialogue.

- What does Grandfather's dialogue suggest about Carmen? *(She is a talented runner.)*
- How does Grandfather's dialogue about Carmen contrast with the dialogue of Carmen's mother? *(Grandfather takes Carmen's running seriously, unlike her mother.)*

Note that in most stories a character changes. Often authors show changes through thoughts, actions, and dialogue.

- Which character changes in "Rush"? *(Carmen)*
- How does the character change? *(Carmen doesn't want to see her grandfather until she remembers her last visit.)*
- How can you tell when her character changes? *(Her thoughts about visiting him change when she remembers his support.)*

If... students have trouble identifying how a character changes,

then... have them identify the character's thoughts, feelings, dialogue, and actions in the beginning and at the end of the story and compare them.

On Their Own As students read "Heatstroke" on Worktext p. 42 independently or with you, have them complete a Four-Column Chart on p. 95. For additional practice, assign p. 43.

Comprehension Lesson 8
Plot

Objectives:

- Identify the plot, or what happens at the beginning, middle, and end of a story.
- Identify the problem and solution in a story.
- Distinguish between important and unimportant plot events.
- Relate the characters' actions to plot development.

MATERIALS

Worktext pp. 44–49
T-Chart, p. 101
Events in a Story Organizer, p. 93
Plot Structure Organizer, p. 97
Leveled Reader Database

Set the scene Explain that the plot is what happens in a story. Tell students that a plot has a beginning, a middle, and an end. Most events in a story are related to a problem and its solution. Readers identify the events of the plot to better understand a story.

Model and teach Read "Bike for Sale" aloud.

Bike for Sale

Every May John's family held a garage sale. John decided to sell old toys and clothes. Then he asked his brother Tom what he was selling.

"Oh, just some old video games and my bike." Tom was almost in high school, so he didn't ride his bike anymore. John looked at his own bike. Maybe he could start walking everywhere like Tom did. He decided to sell his bike too.

At the garage sale, the video games sold fast. Then a neighbor spotted John's bike. "Oh, my grandson would love that," she said, handing John the bills.

That night John felt sad. After dinner, he saw the neighbor boy riding his old bike up the street. He felt like throwing the money at him and taking his bike back.

Later, Tom stopped by. "I can't believe my bike didn't sell!" he said.

John had an idea. "How about $20 for it?"

"Deal!"

Use a T-Chart from p. 101 with columns labeled *Problem* and *Solution* to help students identify the story's conflict. Point out parts of the text as support.

Mini-Lesson 1

Remind students that...

- a plot of a story is made of events that happen one after the other.
- a plot has a beginning, a middle, and an end.
- they can keep track of the order of events to better understand a story.
- a story's plot includes the problem and solution.

Guide Practice

Help students understand that plot events happen in sequential order. They can identify the important plot events to better understand the story.

Ask students to help you find important events in the story "Bike for Sale" and record them in an Events in a Story Organizer from p. 93. Reread the story as necessary. What's the first thing that happens? The first paragraph says that John decides to sell old toys and clothes at the garage sale. What happens next? John talks to Tom and decides to sell his bike. Work together to figure out the other events. Remind students only to include the most important events that affect the outcome of the story.

If... students have trouble keeping track of important events,

then... encourage them to write the events in order in an organizer or list.

On Their Own As students read "Saturday's Party" on Worktext p. 44 independently or with you, have them complete an Events in a Story Organizer to keep track of important events. For additional practice, assign p. 45.

Mini-Lesson 2

Remind students that...
- the plot events occur in sequential order.
- important plot events affect the outcome of the story.
- characters' actions affect plot development.

Guide Practice

Remind students that plot events usually happen in order. What is the correct order for the events in "Bike for Sale" on the previous page? *John wishes he hadn't sold his bike (2); John decides to sell his bike (1); John offers to buy Tom's bike (3).*

Point out that important events affect the overall action in the story, but unimportant events do not. For example, an important event is John's decision to sell his bike. That decision begins the conflict, or problem, that affects the entire story. An unimportant event is that John sells old clothes and toys at the sale. This event does not affect the rest of the plot. Point out that characters have a

definite affect on plot. Their feelings cause them to act, and their actions—such as John's selling of his bike—affect plot.

If... students have trouble distinguishing important and unimportant events,

then... have them first decide if and how an event affects the story's overall action.

 On Their Own As students read "Tornado in Lake County" on Worktext p. 46 independently or with you, have them complete an Events in a Story Organizer from p. 93. For additional practice, assign p. 47.

Mini-Lesson 3

Remind students that...
- a plot includes a conflict, which is resolved at the end of the story.
- the conflict can exist between characters, between a character and an outside force, between groups, or within a character.
- the events of the plot can be organized into the conflict, rising action, climax, and resolution.

Guide Practice

Display a Plot Structure Organizer from p. 97 with labels for *Conflict, Rising Action, Climax,* and *Resolution.* The *conflict* is the problem in the story. Point out that a conflict can occur between characters, between a character and nature, between two groups, or within a character. The *rising action* includes events that build the conflict. The *climax* occurs when the character confronts the conflict directly. The *resolution* is how the conflict is resolved.

Reread "Bike for Sale" from the previous page, and fill in the organizer. What is the conflict? *(John wishes he hadn't sold his bike.)* Who is the conflict between? *(within John)* Have students suggest events in the rising action. What is the climax? *(John sees the neighbor boy and wants to take his bike.)* What is the resolution? *(John buys Tom's bike.)*

If... students have trouble identifying a story's climax,
then... have them identify the point of most tension in the story, just before the resolution.

 On Their Own As students read "The Accident" on Worktext p. 48 independently or with you, have them complete a Plot Structure Organizer. For additional practice, assign p. 49.

Comprehension Lesson 9
Setting

Objectives:
- Identify where and when a story takes place.
- Distinguish between real and imaginary settings.
- Infer the setting from details.
- Determine how setting relates character, plot, and mood.

MATERIALS
Worktext pp. 50–55
Setting of a Story Organizer, p. 98
Leveled Reader Database

Set the scene Explain that the setting is when and where a story takes place. Settings can be either real or make-believe. In some stories, setting is important to the characters and the action of the story. As students read, instruct them to look for details about the setting and think about how it affects the rest of the story.

Model and teach Read aloud "The Flip."

The Flip

Yesterday Kira went fishing with her father. Icy water sprayed her bare arms as the boat slammed against the waves. Kira gripped the railing. The lake spread out for miles. Kira liked fishing, but she was a little afraid of falling out of the boat.

Kira's father turned the boat toward Storm Island, and Kira saw a pair of kayakers. Suddenly a large wave crashed toward the kayakers, and one tipped over. "Oh, no!" cried Kira. "Look!" She held her breath.

"Just wait," said her father.

Just then the kayaker flipped back over with a splash. He was still seated in the boat, holding the paddle. He and his friend had a good laugh. "See?" said Kira's father, smiling. "They're built to flip over." Kira nodded but tightened her life jacket.

Use the Setting of a Story Organizer on p. 98. Where is the story happening? It happens on a boat on a lake. When is it happening? The first sentence says "yesterday." Next, I look for details about setting. The first paragraph says, "the lake spread out for miles," so it must be a big lake. Record this in the organizer and continue modeling.

Remind students that...
- the setting is where and when a story takes place.
- a setting can be real or imaginary.

Guide Practice
Help students understand how to identify where and when a story takes place by giving examples.

- *Last summer, Elsa stayed with her cousins in New York. They lived in an apartment full of books, records, and old furniture.* Where does the story happen? *(in an apartment in New York)* When does it happen? *(last summer)*
- *Raul grew tired of Nebraska. He took a time machine back in history to see what life with dinosaurs was like.* Where does the story happen? *(Nebraska)* When does it happen? *(in the present and during the time of dinosaurs)*

- Which of the stories could be about a real time and place? *(the first story)*
- Which of the stories is about an imaginary time and place? *(the second one)* How do you know? *(The character travels back to the time of dinosaurs, which could not really happen.)*

If... students have trouble identifying setting, **then...** have them reread the text, circling details about place and time.

On Their Own As students read "Juan's Birthday" on Worktext p. 50 independently or with you, have them complete a Setting of a Story Organizer from p. 98. For additional practice, assign p. 51.

Mini-Lesson 2

Remind students that...
- the setting is where and when a story takes place.
- the setting may or may not be stated directly.
- they can infer the setting from details in the story.

Guide Practice
Read aloud "Sailor Days."

Sailor Days

When Grandfather was young, he had been a sailor. On one trip, the wind had died down, and Grandfather and the crew floated lazily mile after mile. The sun blazed. No one saw a cloud, nor even a bit of rock or sand, for weeks.

Model how to figure out the setting when it is not stated directly. What details suggest *when* the story happened? *("When Grandfather was young" suggests it happened in the past.)* What details suggest *where* it happened?

(Details such as being a sailor, floating, and not seeing rock or sand for weeks suggest an ocean setting. The lack of wind and clouds and the blazing sun suggest it was warm.)

If... students have trouble inferring the setting,
then... ask such questions as, "What details give clues about time or age?" and "What details give clues about climate or weather?"

 On Their Own Have students read "Hansel and Gretel" on Worktext p. 52 independently or with you, filling out the Setting of a Story Organizer from p. 98. For additional practice, assign p. 53.

Mini-Lesson 3

Remind students that...
- setting can affect the plot events in a story.
- setting can affect the actions and behaviors of characters in a story.
- details of the setting can reflect the mood of a story.

Guide Practice
Help students understand how setting can affect character, plot, and mood. For example, in a story about survival in the Arctic, characters would probably act and behave differently in the cold setting than in a hot setting.

Reread "The Flip" from the previous page.
- How does the setting affect the action in the story? *(The action involves Kira's boat ride and seeing the kayaker flip. This action is directly related to the lake setting.)*

- How does the setting affect how Kira's character behaves? *(Kira is a bit afraid of the lake, which causes her to worry about the kayaker.)*
- How does the setting affect the overall feeling in the story? *(The overall feeling is suspenseful as a result of Kira's fear of the water.)*

If... students have trouble deciding whether the setting affects the plot or character in a story,
then... have them think about if and how the story would change if the setting were completely different.

 On Their Own Have students read "Saturday on Ice" on Worktext p. 54 independently or with you, using the Setting of a Story Organizer from p. 98. For additional practice, assign p. 55.

Comprehension Lesson 10
Theme

Copyright © Pearson Education, Inc., or its affiliates. All Rights Reserved.

Objectives:

- Recognize the underlying lesson or meaning of a story.
- Distinguish between the subject and the theme of a story.
- Identify both stated and implied themes.
- Support a chosen theme using evidence from the text.

MATERIALS

Worktext pp. 56–61
Story Sequence A Organizer, p. 99
Leveled Reader Database

Set the scene Explain that the theme is the big idea or meaning of a story. To find the theme, students should think about what the author wants the reader to learn. Sometimes the author states the theme directly, but usually readers must infer it.

Model and teach Read aloud "First Day."

First Day

It was the first day of school, and John already had an assignment.

School had been fun all day. His teacher, Miss Miller, was very nice. John had made some new friends and played lots of games. Then at the end of the day Miss Miller asked the class to take out a sheet of paper. John was not happy.

"It's only the first day of class!" John thought worriedly. "How can we have an assignment? How will I do?"

"I will now ask you a question, and you will write your response on your paper," said Miss Miller.

John held his breath. Miss Miller smiled as she said, "The question is: What was your favorite part of school today?"

John breathed a sigh of relief. He would have fun completing this assignment!

Use a Story Sequence A Organizer from p. 99. What did John learn? What he thought was going to be difficult turned out to be fun. What is the theme? *(Sometimes things seem difficult but turn out better than expected.)*

Mini-Lesson 1

Remind students that...

- a story has a big idea or meaning.
- they can figure out the meaning of a story by thinking about what the characters learn.

Guide Practice

Read the story aloud.

Juan and Pete were friends. They had a big test the next day. Juan went home after school. He prepared for the test all evening. Pete went to the park instead. Then he went home and played a game. At last he opened his books. He soon fell asleep. The next day Juan was ready for the test. Pete was tired. He worried he would not do well.

- What happens in the beginning, middle, and end? *(First, the boys have a test tomorrow. Juan studies, but Pete does not. Finally, Juan feels prepared, but Pete is worried.)*

- What does Pete learn? *(By playing instead of studying, he isn't ready for the test.)*
- What is the big idea of the story? *(Studying before a test helps you feel confident and prepared.)*

If... students have trouble identifying theme, **then...** have them think about what the author wants them to learn from the story.

On Their Own As students read "A Little Help" on Worktext p. 56 independently or with you, have them complete a Story Sequence A Organizer from p. 99. For additional practice, assign p. 57.

Mini-Lesson 2

Remind students that...
- a theme is the lesson or meaning of a story.
- some themes are stated directly.
- a theme should be supported by evidence from the text.

Guide Practice
Read the story aloud.

The Science Fair Project

The science fair was next week. Melissa decided to work alone. She did not need anyone's help. When Melissa's sister asked if she needed a hand, Melissa rolled her eyes and said, "No, thanks."

On the night before the fair, Melissa was worried. She still had to record her data and finish her posters. She didn't have time to finish, but now she was too embarrassed to ask for help.

Then Melissa's sister stopped by. "Are you *sure* you don't need help?" This time Melissa accepted. They finished just in time for the fair.

What do you think is the theme? *(Sometimes everyone needs help.)* What evidence from the text supports this theme? *(Melissa thinks she doesn't need help, but then realizes she does. She is embarrassed, but she accepts help when her sister offers again.)*

If... students have trouble determining theme,
then... have them first identify what Melissa learns.

On Their Own Have students read "The Hare and the Tortoise" on Worktext p. 58 independently or with you, filling out the Story Sequence A Organizer from p. 99. For additional practice, assign p. 59.

Mini-Lesson 3

Remind students that...
- the theme is the underlying meaning of a story.
- the theme can be either stated or implied.
- a story can have more than one theme.
- themes recur across different stories, cultures, and time periods.

Guide Practice
Read the story aloud.

The Ants and the Grasshopper

The ants spend each day in the summer gathering grain. A grasshopper hops by, singing to himself. He asks the ants why they are working so hard. They tell the grasshopper that they are gathering food for winter. The grasshopper laughs. "But it's beautiful outside!" he sings. Then he hops away, still singing. When winter comes, the ants have plenty of food. The grasshopper struggles to feed himself until the ants share their food. The grasshopper was very grateful.

- What is one theme of the story? *(Possible response: Prepare now for a better future.)*
- What is another theme of the story? *(Possible response: It is good to help those in need.)*
- Is it stated or implied? *(implied)*

If... students have trouble recognizing more than one theme in the story,
then... have them think about what each main character learns.

On Their Own Have students read "Trouble at the Table" on Worktext p. 60 independently or with you, using the Story Sequence A Organizer from p. 99. For additional practice, assign p. 61.

Comprehension Lesson 11
Retell/Summarize

MATERIALS

Worktext pp. 62–67
Web, p. 104
Routine Cards 15 and 16
Leveled Reader Database

Set the scene Explain retelling and summarizing, emphasizing that each focuses only on main ideas and events. To retell a story, tell the goals of the characters, how they tried to reach those goals, and whether or not they did. To summarize nonfiction, tell only the main ideas in order. Summarizing and retelling help you check your understanding and remember what you've read.

Model and teach Read aloud "Martin Luther King, Jr."

Martin Luther King, Jr.

Martin Luther King, Jr., was an activist in the 1960s. During this time, people were treated differently depending on the color of their skin. Dr. King started giving speeches and marching to protest unfair laws. He was arrested 30 times. Thousands of people listened to Dr. King. They helped him fight to have all people treated the same, regardless of the color of their skin. Dr. King gave one of the most famous speeches in history, "I Have a Dream." He moved people to change the way people of color were treated.

Display and fill in a Web from p. 104. Write the topic, *Dr. King,* in the center oval. First, I figure out the main ideas, or what the article is mostly about. People were treated unfairly; Dr. King protested unfair laws; Dr. King's speeches helped to get all people treated fairly. **Write these in the outer ovals.**

To summarize, I tell only the main ideas: *Dr. King gave speeches and marched to protest unfair laws and treatment. He inspired others to treat all people fairly.*

 **Mini-Lesson 1**

Remind students that...
- retelling a story means telling the goals of the characters, how they tried to reach those goals, and whether or not they reached their goals.
- summarizing nonfiction means telling the important ideas in your own words.

Guide Practice

Tell students to focus only on important events when they retell stories. Ask yourself, "What did the characters want? How did they try to get it? Were they successful?" Read the story aloud, and ask students to retell it.

Our Garden

My sister Ana and I planted flowers in our garden. First, we dug many holes in the soil. Then we put some seeds in each hole. We watered them every day. Soon, the flowers began to grow. The flowers made our yard look very pretty.

What did the girls want? *(They wanted to plant flowers in their garden.)* How did they try to get it? *(They planted seeds and watered them.)* Were they successful? *(Yes.)*

If... students have trouble retelling events in order, **then...** use Routine Card 15 and have them figure out what happens next, and last.

 On Their Own As students read "My Uncle, the Firefighter" on Worktext p. 62 independently or with you, have them complete a Web from p. 104 to practice retelling a story. For practice summarizing nonfiction, assign p. 63.

Mini-Lesson 2

Remind students that...

- retelling a story means telling the goals of the characters, how they tried to reach those goals, and whether or not they reached their goals.
- a summary tells only the most important ideas or events in order.
- summaries should only be a few sentences.

Guide Practice

Remind students that summaries of nonfiction selections, such as articles, include only the main ideas. A summary does not include unnecessary details, and it should be shorter than the original selection. If students need to review main ideas and details, revisit Lesson 4. Reread "Martin Luther King, Jr." on the previous page. Then read aloud the two summaries below.

Summary 1: Dr. King was an activist who gave the "I Have a Dream" speech.

Summary 2: Dr. King gave speeches to protest unfair laws and treatment. His famous speeches inspired others to treat all people fairly.

Which is the best summary? *(Summary 2)* Why? *(It includes only the most important ideas. Summary 1 includes details rather than main ideas.)*

If... students have trouble identifying why one summary is better than the other,

then... use Routine Card 16 and ask, "What is the selection about?" and "What are the most important parts?"

On Their Own To practice retelling a story, have students read "A Great Chef" on Worktext p. 64 independently or with you, and have them fill out a Web from p. 104. For practice summarizing, assign p. 65.

Mini-Lesson 3

Remind students that...

- retelling a story means telling the goals of the characters, how they tried to reach those goals, and whether or not they reached their goals.
- a summary tells only the main ideas or events in order.
- they can use text structure to help determine how to summarize a selection.

Guide Practice

Read aloud "Guide Dogs."

Guide Dogs

To become a guide dog, a dog first goes to training school. Guide dogs learn how to listen, walk around people, lead, and use stairs. Next, they learn how to safely cross streets by watching traffic. When guide dogs finish training, they are placed with owners.

How are the details in the article organized? *(sequence order, or the order in which they happen)* Summarize "Guide Dogs." *(Possible answer: Guide dogs go to training school to learn skills to help their owners get around safely. After training, they are placed with owners.)* Point out that a good summary of "Guide Dogs" includes the main ideas in sequence order.

If... students have trouble identifying text structure,

then... use Routine Card 16 and have students ask themselves, "What are the most important ideas?" and "What is discussed first, next, and last?"

On Their Own To practice retelling, have students read "Sick Day" on Worktext p. 66 independently or with you. Have them use the Web from p. 104. For practice summarizing, assign p. 67.

Comprehension Lesson 12
Background Knowledge

Objectives:
- Recognize background knowledge while reading.
- Use background knowledge to connect to a new story or article.
- Use background knowledge to monitor understanding while reading.
- Develop and use background knowledge related to genre.

MATERIALS
Worktext pp. 68–73
Three-Column Chart, p. 102
T-Chart, p. 101
Leveled Reader Database

Set the scene Tell students that background knowledge is what they already know about a topic through their own experiences or other readings. For example, they might have done something similar to what a character in a story does. Or, they might read about a topic that they have read about before.

Model and teach First, display a Three-Column Chart from p. 102. Set it up as a KWL Chart. What do you already know about elephants? What do you want to know? Then read the article aloud.

The Biggest Land Animals
Elephants are the biggest animals on land. An adult elephant can be 12,000 pounds! A baby elephant is about 200 pounds when it is born. It gains 2 pounds a day.

Elephants spend sixteen hours a day finding plants. They like to eat grass and leaves. Sometimes they eat fruit and flowers.

Each elephant has a long trunk. Elephants can use their trunk to carry water and to reach food. They also use their trunks to "shake hands" with other elephants.

Elephants have big families and are very social. In addition, elephants are very smart. They can use tools, play games, paint pictures, and even laugh.

Help students fill in the rest of the chart. Point out how students' background knowledge helped them connect to and understand the article.

Mini-Lesson 1

Remind students that...
- their background knowledge is what they already know about something.
- using background knowledge helps them connect to what they read.

Guide Practice
Read the story aloud.

Ben's Gift
Ben wants to get a birthday gift for his mother. He goes to the store with his father.

After a while, Ben sees a pretty red hat. "She might like that," thinks Ben. Then he sees a dress with flowers. His mother likes flowers.

Ben looks at his money. "I don't think you have enough for the dress," says Ben's father. "Let's keep looking."

They look, but Ben cannot find the right gift. His father drives him home. Ben feels sad.

Ben walks through the yard alone. He sees a bright red flower. "I know what to give her!" he says.

Help students connect to the story. Why is Ben upset? *(He can't find the right gift.)* When have you felt like Ben? What other stories does this remind you of?

If... students have trouble making connections, **then...** ask questions such as, "What does this remind you of in your own life?"

On Their Own As students read "One Last Thing" on Worktext p. 68 independently or with you, have them complete a T-Chart from p. 101 to connect the story to their own lives. For additional practice, assign p. 69.

Mini-Lesson 2

Remind students that...
- using background knowledge helps them connect to what they read.
- they can compare new texts to texts they have already read to better understand them.

Guide Practice
Reread the article on the previous page. Then read aloud the passage below.

Elephants: Symbol of Thailand

Elephants have been important to the people of Thailand for centuries. They live in Thailand's jungles. People have used elephants for farming, traveling, and fighting wars.

Thai people believe that rare white elephants are special animals. White elephants are often given to kings and treated with honor.

Today there are more people and fewer wild elephants in Thailand. Some people hunt them illegally. Some people bring elephants to cities to beg for money. Yet others work to protect the animals.

Based on the first article, why do you think Thai people used elephants for farming, traveling, and royalty? *(They are large, strong, smart, and social.)* Why do you think elephants are a problem in cities? *(They are large and possibly destructive; they cannot find enough food.)*

If... students have trouble applying background knowledge,
then... first ask, "What about the first article reminds you of the second article?"

On Their Own As students read "The Truth About Spiders" on Worktext p. 70 independently or with you, have them fill out a Three-Column Chart from p. 102. For additional practice, assign p. 71.

Mini-Lesson 3

Remind students that...
- they can use background knowledge to connect to and better understand stories or articles.
- they can develop and use background knowledge related to genre.

Guide Practice
Copy the article on the board and read it aloud.

Thailand Fights Elephant Begging

BANGKOK, Thailand—A man walked his elephant through the streets, begging for money to feed him. Today there are more than 100 elephants used like this in the city.

Elephant Begging

It is against the law to bring elephants into the city. Yet many people use elephants to beg for money. Both the animals and the city suffer.

A New Plan

Today people in Thailand are fighting to keep elephants out of the city. They started a plan to buy the elephants from their owners. Then they will release them into the wild.

What type of writing is this? *(article)* Is if nonfiction or fiction? *(nonfiction)* Based on what you know about nonfiction articles, what do you expect to read about? *(facts and current events)*

If... students have trouble applying background knowledge,
then... have them ask, "What do I already know about this topic and genre?" as they read.

On Their Own Have students read "India's Taj Mahal" on Worktext p. 72, independently or with you, and use a Three-Column Chart from p. 102. For additional practice, assign p. 73.

Comprehension Lesson 13
Questioning

Objectives:
- Ask questions before, during, and after reading.
- Ask and answer questions in a story or passage that tell *who, what, when, where, why,* and *how.*
- Ask and answer questions to activate prior knowledge, discover meaning, monitor comprehension, and make predictions.

MATERIALS
Worktext pp. 74–79
Three-Column Chart, p. 102
Leveled Reader Database

Set the scene Explain that students should ask questions before, during, and after reading to keep track of what they read. For example, when you read a story, keep track of who the characters are, what they do and why, and how things happen. Note also where and when the story occurs. For articles, ask questions about the most important information. To answer questions, read or reread the text.

Model and teach Display a Three-Column Chart from Worktext p. 102 and set it up as a KWL Chart. To understand a new story, I record what I know and what I want to learn in a chart. First, I preview the story. This story is called "The Homework Assignment." Write this in the *K* column. In the *W* column, write questions such as, *Who are the characters? What happens?* and so on. Then read the story aloud.

The Homework Assignment
Mrs. Garcia asked, "Kyle, where is your math homework?"

I looked in my backpack. Where was it? I worked for hours finishing the multiplication problems last night. My palms were beginning to sweat.

My mom had checked the work. We even laughed when she made a mistake that I caught! I remember Dad called us to come to dinner. I closed the book and packed my bag.

That was it! I opened my math book, and there it was, tucked between the pages. Boy, was I relieved!

After reading, record answers to the questions in the *L* column and continue modeling.

Mini-Lesson 1

Remind students that...
- they can ask questions before, during, and after they read.
- asking and answering *who, what, when, where, why,* and *how* questions will help them understand what they read.
- they should read and reread the text to answer any remaining questions.

Guide Practice
Give students practice questioning.
- Yesterday, Paul was supposed to run in a race. When he got to the race, his friend Joe said it was canceled because of the rain.

What questions could you ask? (*Who is in the story? What happens?*) Then have students answer their questions. (*Paul and Joe are characters. Their race is canceled.*)

- Young kangaroos are born when they are very small. With their claws, they crawl up their mother's fur to get inside her pouch. There the young grow.

What *why* and *how* questions could you ask? (*Why do young kangaroos need to get to their mother's pouch? How do they get there?*) How would you answer them? (*They grow in the pouch. They crawl up their mother.*)

If... students have trouble identifying which questions to ask,

then... remind them of the 5 Ws and H: *who, what, where, when, why,* and *how.*

On Their Own As students read "Socks" on Worktext p. 74 independently or with you, have them complete a Three-Column Chart from p. 102. For additional practice, assign p. 75.

Mini-Lesson 2

Remind students that...
- they can ask questions before, during, and after reading.
- they can ask and answer questions to discover meaning and monitor comprehension.

Guide Practice
Read "Death Valley" aloud.

Death Valley

The hottest, driest, and lowest part in the United States is Death Valley in California. Death Valley gets its name from settlers who came across it while moving to California. The hot, dry valley made the trip dangerous.

In the late 1800s, settlers found gold and other minerals in the mountains near the valley. People moved near the valley for mining and started small towns. Yet once the minerals were gone, people left the towns too.

Guide students to stop and ask questions before, during, and after they read to check comprehension. For example, I ask questions about anything confusing. Which words are new to me? (*Possible answer: settlers, minerals*) How can I find out the meaning of these words? (*Use a dictionary.*) Then I ask, "What is the article mostly about?"

If... students have trouble remembering questions to ask after they read,
then... encourage them to ask questions during reading and answer them before continuing.

 On Their Own As students read "Trip to Grandma's" on Worktext p. 76 independently or with you, have them fill out the Three-Column Chart from p. 102. For additional practice, assign p. 77.

Mini-Lesson 3

Remind students that...
- they can ask and answer questions to activate prior knowledge and make predictions.
- they can answer their questions by rereading parts of the text.

Guide Practice
Read "The Necklace" aloud.

The Necklace

Tina's friend Maya received a shiny new necklace for her birthday and wore it to school. Tina could not take her eyes off that necklace. It had icy, blue stones that caught the light. It was beautiful. She had asked for that same necklace for her birthday, but her mother said it cost too much.

One day Tina was walking home and she saw something in the grass. It was the blue necklace! Tina put it in her pocket.

Then Tina wondered if it belonged to Maya. Maya would be worried if she lost it.

Remind students to come up with their own questions, answers, and predictions as they read the text. For example, they can ask, "How does Tina feel about Maya's necklace? How does Tina feel when she finds a necklace in the grass?" Then tell students that they can ask questions about what will happen next in a story, such as "What do you predict Tina will do next?"

If... students have trouble answering their questions,
then... have them find the answers by rereading the text.

 On Their Own Have students read "First Day of School" on Worktext p. 78 independently or with you, using a Three-Column Chart from p. 102. For additional practice, assign p. 79.

Comprehension Lesson 14
Important Ideas

Objectives:
- Recognize important ideas in a text.
- Distinguish important ideas from minor details.
- Look for important ideas in the text, titles, bold words, visuals, facts, and details.
- Recognize facts and details that support important ideas in the text.

MATERIALS

Worktext pp. 80–85
Web, p. 104
Leveled Reader Database

Set the scene Tell students that it is hard to remember all of the details in a passage, but they should focus on the important ideas. Important ideas are those they need to know to understand the passage. Tell students to look for important ideas in the text, titles, bold words, and graphic sources.

Model and teach Read the article aloud.

Dolphins: Underwater Mammals

Dolphins are born and live underwater. They have fins and swim. They look like fish, but they are not fish. They are mammals. Like other mammals, dolphins breathe air and are warm-blooded. They give birth to live babies.

Baby dolphins can see, hear, and swim from the moment they are born. The baby dolphins can "speak" to their mothers by making whistling noises.

Dolphins eat fish. Baby dolphins don't have teeth, so they can't eat fish. They drink their mother's milk. Baby dolphins stay by their mothers for three to six years. As they grow, baby dolphins learn what to eat. They also have fun playing in the water.

Fill in a Web from p. 104. First, I ask, "What is the article about?" The title tells me that it's about dolphins. Then I look for important ideas. The first paragraph says that dolphins are underwater mammals and explains how they are born. Most of the article tells about baby dolphins. Those are important ideas.

Mini-Lesson 1

Remind students that...
- important ideas are the major ideas in a text.
- titles, bold words, and graphic sources give clues to important ideas.
- some ideas are important, and others are minor.

Guide Practice

Focus on helping students identify important ideas. Practice with the paragraph below. Read it aloud.

How to Adopt a Pet

If you want to adopt a pet, go to the animal shelter. It is open six days a week from 9:00 to 6:00. Right now there are ten dogs, eight cats, and a rabbit. When you go to the shelter, give your name and telephone number to the person at the front desk. They will help you pick out your pet.

- What is this paragraph about? *(how to adopt a pet from the animal shelter)*
- What is important to know? *(when the shelter is open and how to adopt a pet)*
- What is not important to know? *(There are ten dogs, eight cats, and one rabbit.)*
- Why are these details not important? *(They don't help you understand the paragraph.)*

If... students have trouble identifying important ideas,
then... reread sentence-by-sentence and determine whether each sentence has an important idea or not.

On Their Own As students read "Getting a Puppy" on Worktext p. 80 independently or with you, have them complete a Web from p. 104. For additional practice, assign p. 81.

Mini-Lesson 2

Remind students that...
- important ideas are the major ideas in a text.
- some ideas are important, and others are minor.
- they can use facts and details to help identify and support important ideas.

Guide Practice
Read the article aloud.

The Hippopotamus: On Land, In Water

Hippopotamus means "river horse." Hippos are the second-largest land animals. Only elephants are bigger than hippos. Hippos spend a lot of time in lakes and rivers. They are good swimmers.

Hippos enjoy lying in the sun for hours. Sun can dry out their skin quickly. Also, hippos cannot sweat. They need the water to keep their skin wet and cool. Their eyes, ears, and nostrils are high on their head. This allows them to see, hear, and breathe, even while mostly underwater.

- What is the article about? *(hippos' life on land and in water)*
- What is important to know? *(Hippos need to spend a lot of time in water.)*
- What facts and details support these ideas? *(Hippos cannot sweat, and their skin dries out easily.)*

If... students have trouble identifying important ideas, **then...** have them first identify facts and details.

On Their Own Have students read "Lunch at Aunt Hilda's" on Worktext p. 82 independently or with you, using the Web from p. 104. For additional practice, assign p. 83.

Mini-Lesson 3

Remind students that...
- important ideas are the major ideas in a text.
- important ideas are supported by facts and details in the rest of the text.
- important ideas can help them determine the author's purpose for writing a text.

Guide Practice
Read the article aloud.

Your Own Garden

Planting a garden is fun and easy. Gardens need your help to grow. First, choose a sunny place. Gardens do best when plants get enough sun and water.

Next, choose your plants and buy seeds. For best results, choose plants that grow well in the climate where you live.

Then prepare the soil so your plants grow well. Dig a small hole for each seed, and put a seed inside it. Cover the seeds with soil. Water your garden, and soon your plants will start to grow!

- What details are in the first paragraph? *(You need to choose a sunny place, and gardens need water.)*
- What important ideas do they support? *(Gardens need your help to get enough sun and water.)* Repeat for the other paragraphs.
- Why do you think the author wrote the article? *(probably to inform readers)*

If... students have trouble identifying important ideas, **then...** remind them to ask themselves why the author might have written the passage.

On Their Own Have students read "The Moon" on Worktext p. 84 independently or with you, using the Web from p. 104. For additional practice, assign p. 85.

Comprehension Lesson 15
Visualize

Objectives:
- Visualize a story, or create a mental picture of it.
- Use prior knowledge to help picture a story.
- Identify descriptive details that help readers visualize a story.

MATERIALS
Worktext pp. 86–91
Five-Column Chart, p. 94
Leveled Reader Database

Set the scene Explain that when readers visualize a passage, they create a picture of it in their minds. They use what they already know and combine it with details from the text. They use all five senses to see what is happening: smell the smells, hear the sounds, and so on. Visualizing will also help students better remember and enjoy what they read.

Model and teach Read the passage aloud. Have students close their eyes to picture it in their minds.

To the City

Maria stepped off the train. It was her first time in the city. She took a deep breath and followed the crowd out through the noisy station. Outside, the sun made her squint. The dry July heat pressed against her and almost took her breath away. The smell of exhaust caught in her throat. Maria coughed and kept walking. Yellow taxis darted in and out of traffic, honking, stopping to pick up and drop off passengers. At last Maria saw Bridge Street, the sign she was looking for. She shifted her heavy bag on her shoulder and wiped sweat from her forehead. Just eleven more blocks to go, she thought.

After reading, have students open their eyes. Display a Five-Column Chart from p. 94 with each sense listed as a chart head. *What did you see in your mind as you heard the passage? I saw a train station full of people, a sunny day outside the station, and a street congested with taxis. I write these in the chart under* Sight. *Then I can draw pictures to help me remember.* **Continue modeling with the other senses.**

Mini-Lesson 1

Remind students that...
- to visualize means to create a mental picture.
- they can combine what they know with what the author describes to visualize a passage in their minds.

Guide Practice
Have students close their eyes and picture each passage as you read it aloud.

- Ella parted the thorny raspberry bushes. The red berries stained her hand when she picked them, and they tasted cool and sweet.

What did you picture in your mind? (the red raspberries, Ella's stained hands) What do you already know about picking raspberries? What senses helped you picture the text? (touch, sight, and taste)

- Juan waited for his grandmother in her old car. Crumpled newspapers covered the floor. The windows were scratched, and the seats smelled dry and stale.

What did you picture in your mind? (newspapers on the floor, scratched windows) What does the car remind you of in your own life? What senses helped you visualize the text? (sight and smell)

If... students have trouble identifying which senses are engaged,
then... discuss individual details, pointing out clue words, such as *tasted* and *smelled*.

On Their Own Have students read "At the Farm" on Worktext p. 86 independently or with you. For additional practice, assign p. 87 and have them complete the Five-Column Chart.

Mini-Lesson 2

Remind students that...

- to visualize means to create a picture in the mind.
- as they read, they can refine and revise what they visualize to match the author's descriptions in the text.

Guide Practice

Read aloud the story beginning below.

Kate's mom took her to the salon for a haircut. Kate had long, smooth, brown hair. Her mom said short haircuts were best for summer, but Kate did not agree. She just wanted a trim. Once Kate was in the chair, her mom said something to the stylist. The stylist turned Kate away from the mirror. Kate heard snipping and saw long pieces of hair fall to the floor.

What do you picture? *(Kate getting a short haircut.)* Finish the story.

After the stylist finished, she showed Kate the mirror. Her hair was still long! Then she saw her mom in the next chair. Her mom's hair was short and spiky. It was her mom's hair on the floor!

How did your picture change? *(The short haircut changed from Kate to her mom.)*

If... students have trouble identifying how the story changed,
then... have them compare their initial visualization to what they pictured later.

On Their Own Have students read "Young Paul Bunyan" on Worktext p. 88 independently or with you. For additional practice, assign p. 89 and have students fill out the Five-Column Chart from p. 94.

Mini-Lesson 3

Remind students that...

- they can use all five senses to visualize the text.
- they can identify imagery and sensory details to help them visualize the text.

Guide Practice

Read the text aloud.

The New House

Joy looked at the new house. A swing painted bright white hung on the porch. Inside, the kitchen was pale yellow with smooth wooden counters. Joy could hear the willow tree blowing in the breeze in the yard. Inside the living room, the wood floors looked shiny and smooth. As she walked, Joy slid her hand against the rough brick walls. She went upstairs and found her own room. It was not big, but it was bright. Joy sat down on her bed and breathed in the crisp scent of freshly washed sheets.

Display a Five-Column Chart from p. 94 and use each sense as a chart heading. Have students identify the descriptive details that describe each sense and record them in the correct column.

If... students have trouble identifying specific descriptive details,
then... record the text on the board, help students circle each detail, and have them identify the sense each describes.

On Their Own Have students read "The Giant and the Villagers" on Worktext p. 90 independently or with you. For additional practice, assign p. 91 and have students complete the Five-Column Chart.

Comprehension
Student Worktext

Name _____

Read the article.

Mysterious Cicadas
by Chen Lee

I sat outside one evening in May. At last, spring had come. Flowers on the apple tree had opened. The white flowers covered the branches. Their sweet smell hung in the warm air. Then I heard it. The low sound started soft. Then it became loud. Then it became soft again before starting over. It was almost like music. I had never heard a sound like it.

The sound had come from cicadas. Cicadas are a kind of insect. The cicadas I heard that night are a special kind. They live underground for 17 years!

2 Author's Purpose

Name _____

Read the article.

Bear Lake: 2059
by Jon Franks

Imagine Bear Lake many years from now.

The blue water is now brown and thick. No birds sing in the trees. The only sound is the strange wet garbage that pours in. Fish left for clean water years ago. Nothing lives in Bear Lake. Old bottles lie in the grass. People do not picnic at Bear Lake. It is not safe to swim here now.

Do you want this to happen to Bear Lake? We need to stop polluting it. We need to clean it up. Help protect our lake while we still can. It is not too late.

Directions Read "Bear Lake: 2059" with your child. Ask, "Why do you think the author wrote this?" Then ask, "How can you tell?" Make sure your child supports his or her response with evidence from the text.

Comprehension Lesson 1   Author's Purpose **3**

Name _____

Read the article.

Mountain Lions Back in the Midwest?
by Julio Gomez

Al Brown's usual trip to the store last week took a strange turn. Brown was at a stoplight when he saw a mountain lion crossing Golf Road near Lake Michigan. The five-foot-long brown cat walked calmly across the busy road. Cars stopped. People watched in shock. Then the cat disappeared into the woods. "I knew what it was," said Brown. "I just could not believe it!"

Mountain lions live in western states. About 100 years ago, they were hunted out of states in the East and Midwest. Recently, people have seen the cats as far east as Chicago and Boston. Mountain lions are growing in number because the deer they eat are also growing in number. The more cats there are, the more space they need. Yet many people are uneasy about the cats' return.

Directions Have your child read "Mountain Lions Back in the Midwest?" aloud. Ask, "What do you think are the author's purposes for writing this?" Then ask, "What clues in the text helped you figure out the author's purposes?"

4 Author's Purpose

Comprehension Lesson 1

Read the article.

Mount Vesuvius
by Rosa Hernandez

First, the ground shook. Then the top of the mountain opened, and a cloud of hot gas and smoke shot into the sky. Ash, stones, and burning rocks rained down from the cloud. The blanket of ash covered buildings and fields. The cloud blocked the sun, and rocks crashed down, beating holes into the ground. Burning rocks and ash set fire to homes. Soon the whole city was red with flames. People tried to cover their faces as they choked on ash and smoke. Babies cried, and people shouted for help. The smell of sulfur hung in the streets.

No one lived through the eruption of the volcano Mount Vesuvius in the year 79. Everyone was buried under the ash and rock for more than 500 years. When people dug up the site, they found that much of the city was preserved in the ash-like cement. The remains are a frightening reminder of the volcano's power.

Directions Have your child read "Mount Vesuvius" aloud. Ask, "Why do you think the author wrote this?" Remind your child that authors may write for more than one purpose. Then ask, "What clues in the text helped you figure out the author's purposes?"

Read the story.

Neighbors
by Nora Weiss

There was an old house on the corner. No one had lived there for years. Then an old lady parked a truck filled with old furniture out front. It seemed she was moving in. A week went by. When new people moved in, Maria's mother always baked them a cake and introduced herself. Maria's mother was busy, so Maria baked a cake and brought it over.

Maria knocked on the door. The porch was almost rotted through. Overgrown bushes scratched her legs as she waited. No one answered. Maria knocked again. Still no one answered. Maria had second thoughts. Maybe she should not have come. She looked down the road. The old truck was gone.

Just then, Mrs. Jones from across the street walked over. Maria knew of Mrs. Jones, but she had never met her. Maria asked about the lady that had moved in. "Oh, Mrs. Hill?" said Mrs. Jones. "She was just here to clean up the place. She drove home yesterday."

"Well, I have this cake," said Maria. "I was going to introduce myself."

"Oh?" said Mrs. Jones. "Well, my name is Ruth Jones. You must be Maria." Maria smiled. She cut a slice of cake for each of them.

Directions Have your child read "Neighbors" aloud. Ask, "What do you think is the author's purpose or purposes for writing this?" and "How can you tell?" Then ask, "How well do you think the author achieved her purpose?"

Name _____

Read the article.

The Dead Sea
by Jerome Davidson

The blue pool of water stretched out for miles. By the beach, the water lapped quietly. The air smelled salty, like the ocean. There were no trees or grass growing near the water. No seaweed wrapped around the shore. There were people swimming, but no one was fishing. "There are no fish here," people told me. I dipped my foot in.

This is no ordinary sea. In fact, it is not a sea at all.

The Dead Sea is a salt lake in the Middle East with land on all sides. It is about 394 square miles and about 1,000 feet deep. The Dead Sea is the lowest body of water on Earth. Small streams, springs, and the Jordan River empty water into the sea, but no water drains out of it. When water evaporates, salt is left behind. As more water pours into the Dead Sea, the water brings more and more salt. The sea is now about nine times as salty as the oceans! That much salt will kill almost any living thing, such as fish. The salt does not hurt people. In fact, the salt in the water makes it easier to float!

Directions Have your child read "The Dead Sea" aloud. Ask, "What do you think is the author's purpose or purposes for writing this?" and "How can you tell?" Then ask, "Did the author achieve his purpose?" and "Why or why not?"

Name _____

Read the paragraph.

A New Life

The Jones family moved to River Falls last year. Sometimes they think about moving back to their old town. They think about moving because they miss their family. They also miss their old friends. Yet the Jones family is happy in River Falls. They're happy because they own a small store and have a lot of customers. They also live in a nice house. They're also happy because they have many friends.

Directions Read "A New Life" with your child. Then have your child circle the cause-effect clue words. Ask, "The Jones family is happy in River Falls. What are three causes for that?"

Name _____

Read the story.

Trip to the Zoo

Kim was Jen's best friend. Kim had moved last year, so Jen did not see her much now.

Jen invited Kim to stay with her. They planned to go to the zoo. Jen knew Kim loved the animals. Kim liked monkeys best of all. She liked how the baby monkeys chased each other. She also liked when they jumped from tree to tree.

Kim came, and Jen took her to the zoo. Jen saw the sign first. Oh no! The monkey house was closed for cleaning! Jen thought Kim would be sad. Kim wasn't sad because she was just glad to see Jen. The two girls saw other animals and had a fun day.

School + Home

Directions Read "Trip to the Zoo" with your child. Ask, "Jen invites Kim to stay with her. What causes her to do this?" Then ask, "Why wasn't Kim sad about the monkey house being closed?"

Name _____

Read the article.

Changes

People move to other countries for many different reasons. Sometimes a person can get a better education in another country. Sometimes people move because they find a better job in another country. Many times, they help people in their new country.

When Ilona was 7 years old, she moved to the United States from Poland. Her family had decided it was time for a change. Her father, David, wanted to help people who were hurt or sick. He got a good job at a hospital. Her mother, Sophie, went to business school. She wanted to start her own business. Ilona went to an American school. She learned how to speak English, but she never forgot how to speak Polish.

Today Ilona teaches American children how to speak Polish. David helps older people stay healthy. Sophie started her own business. She helps young people find jobs.

School + Home

Directions Have your child read "Changes" aloud. Ask, "According to the article, what are two causes for moving to another country?" and "What are three effects of Ilona's family moving to the United States?"

Comprehension Lesson 2

Name _____

Read the article.

Women's Right to Vote

For many years, only men could vote. Men voted for the president and for other members of government. Men voted for the people who would make the changes they wanted. Women wanted changes too. Yet they could not vote to make those changes happen.

Women became angry because they could not vote. They said it was unfair. They joined groups and made speeches. They fought for many years because they too wanted the right to vote.

Some places, such as Wyoming, allowed women to vote. As these places became states, more people supported women's right to vote. In 1920, the U.S. government had to decide whether women from all states should have the right to vote. Harry Burns from Tennessee made the deciding vote. People thought Burns would vote against women. But his mother had given him a note that told him to "be a good boy." Burns voted for women's right to vote, so the decision became the law.

Directions Have your child read "Women's Right to Vote" aloud. Ask, "What are two reasons, or causes, that women fought for the right to vote?" Then ask, "Why do you think some people may have fought against giving women the right to vote?"

Read the story.

A Birthday Surprise

Sandra and Janet have been best friends since first grade. Because they have the same birthday, they have a birthday party together every year. Their parents plan the party and invite all their friends.

This year was a little different. Both girls felt they were old enough to plan their own party, and they wanted to do something special. Sandra wanted to give Janet a surprise party. As a result, she invited all their friends and family. Since the weather was hot and Janet likes to swim, Sandra planned a beach party. Her parents thought it was a wonderful idea. Sandra told everyone to bring bathing suits and beach balls. She made a sign that said "Happy Birthday Janet!"

Janet wanted to give Sandra a surprise party too. Sandra likes to find seashells. So Janet planned a beach party too. She told the same friends and family whom Sandra had invited. Janet wondered why everyone giggled when she invited them. She made a sign that said "Happy Birthday Sandra!" and decorated it with seashells.

On the day of the parties, Sandra and Janet went to the beach. All their friends and family were there, and they shouted, "Surprise!" Sandra and Janet both thought the other friend would be surprised. Then they saw their signs and burst out laughing.

Happy Birthday Sandra!

School + Home

Directions Ask your child to read aloud "A Birthday Surprise." Have your child circle the cause-effect clue words. Then read those sentences aloud together. For each sentence, ask your child, "What's the effect in this sentence?" and "What caused that effect?"

Name _____

Read the article.

The Truth About Sharks

Many people are afraid of sharks. Because of their fear, some people do not care when people kill the animals. Yet shark attacks happen less often than many people think.

Sharks attack a very small number of people each year. Around the world, fewer than 80 shark attacks happen each year. Only about 10 of those people die each year because of attacks. It is true that the number of shark attacks has grown in the past 100 years. This is because today more people spend more time in oceans where sharks live. In the past 10 years, however, the number of sharks has started to fall. Therefore, there are even fewer attacks than before.

The drop in the number of sharks hurts oceans. Hunting and fishing kill thousands of sharks every year. Many countries hunt sharks for soup. As a result, some kinds of sharks may die out. Sharks are important to oceans because they eat weak and sick fish. This helps keep the ocean water healthy. It also helps keep numbers of other fish from getting too high. Killing sharks often causes more harm than good.

Directions Ask your child to read aloud "The Truth About Sharks." Have your child circle the cause-effect clue words. Then read those sentences aloud together. For each sentence, ask your child, "What's the effect in this sentence?" and "What caused that effect?"

Name _____

Read the story.

Blue and Eddie

Dan walked his dog Blue. Blue was unlike other dogs in the neighborhood. Blue was big. He used to be a racing dog. Dan did not care how fast Blue could run. Both Dan and Blue liked going on long walks.

During their walk, Dan saw his friend Frank. Frank was also with his dog. His dog was named Eddie. Both Eddie and Blue were friendly dogs. But Eddie was tiny. He was so small that sometimes Frank put him in his bike basket. Eddie lifted his head. His ears blew back in the wind. Eddie liked riding in the basket better than walking.

Directions Read the story with your child. Ask, "What does this story remind you of in your own life?" Then ask, "How are Blue and Eddie alike?" and "How are they different?"

Name _____

Read the story.

Something for Everyone

Carla went to the park. She brought her sister Ann and her brother Joe. At the park, Carla saw her neighbor. They both liked to play chess. They played on the tables under the trees.

At the park, Ann saw her friends. They chased each other on the grass. Ann could run very fast. No one could catch her.

Joe brought his paints to the park. He also brought some paper. He liked to paint outside. Joe painted Ann and her friends. Then he painted Carla winning at chess.

School + Home

Directions Read "Something for Everyone" with your child. Ask, "What does this story remind you of in your own life?" Then ask, "Which characters in the story are alike, and how?" and "How are they different?"

Read the story.

Summer Camp

Pete and Fred are best friends. Both of them were excited to go to camp for the summer. Pete had gone to camp last year. He had made friends from all over the state. He was excited to see how his camp friends had changed since last year. Pete was also excited for the swimming races and diving contests. He had improved a lot since last year.

Unlike Pete, this was Fred's first time at camp. Fred was excited to meet new people. He also wanted to learn how to canoe. Like Pete, Fred was excited for the swimming and diving. Both boys had taken swimming lessons that year.

Pete and Fred both loved the outdoors. But Fred was worried about bee stings and bear attacks. Pete said there was nothing to worry about. One of the camp counselors was a nurse, he said. All the singing and talking would scare any bears away. Secretly, though, Pete was a little afraid of bears too.

Directions Have your child read the story aloud. Then have him or her circle the comparison and contrast clue words. Ask, "How are Pete's and Fred's excitement about camp similar?" and "How are their past camp experiences different?" Then ask, "How are their feelings about the outdoors similar and different?"

Name _____

Read the article.

Atlantic and Pacific Salmon

Salmon is a type of fish found in both fresh water and salt water. Two main kinds of salmon are Atlantic and Pacific salmon.

Both Atlantic and Pacific salmon lay eggs in fresh water. After the young are born, they swim downstream to salt water. There they grow into adults. The salmon swim back to fresh water to lay eggs. Both Atlantic and Pacific salmon swim to the exact place where they were born to lay their eggs. Some kinds of salmon swim up to 2,000 miles.

Atlantic salmon return each year to lay eggs. Pacific salmon are often bigger than Atlantic salmon. Many kinds of Pacific salmon also swim farther than Atlantic salmon to lay their eggs.

School + Home

Directions Have your child read the article aloud. Then have him or her circle the comparison and contrast clue words. Ask, "What are two ways Atlantic and Pacific salmon are alike?" and "What are two ways they are different?"

Name _____

Read the stories.

Ye Xian

There is a woman named Ye Xian. She has a mean
stepmother. She also has a mean stepsister. They make her clean
all day. One day Ye Xian sees a fish in the river. It is the spirit of
her dead mother. Her mean family eats the fish. Then the spirit
comes again. She tells her daughter to put the fish bones in a pot
under her bed.

The family plans a big party. Ye Xian cannot go. Then she
looks under the bed. A beautiful dress is in the pot. A pair of
golden slippers is also in the pot. She puts them on. She goes
to the party. She has a great time. Then she leaves. She loses a
slipper on the way. The King finds it. He says he will marry the
woman whose foot fits into the slipper. Ye Xian puts it on. The
slipper fits, and they get married.

Cinderella

Cinderella has a mean stepmother. She also has two mean
stepsisters. They make her clean all day. The Prince asks all the
women in the land to a ball. Cinderella has no nice clothes. She is
not allowed to go. She cries in her room. Then a Fairy Godmother
appears. She turns rags into a beautiful dress. She makes the girl a
pair of glass slippers. Cinderella goes to the ball. There the Prince
falls in love with her.

Directions Have your child read the stories aloud. Ask, "How are the stories about Ye Xian
and Cinderella alike?" and "How are they different?"

Comprehension Lesson 3

Name _____

Read the articles.

The Galveston Storm of 1900

On September 8, 1900, a hurricane crashed into Galveston. The storm had hit Cuba a few days before. Winds and rain destroyed many cities in Cuba. People warned about the dangers of the storm. Yet people in Galveston were not worried. They were told to leave the island city. Still, most people stayed.

On the morning of the storm, heavy rains poured down. At last, people tried to leave their homes to move to higher ground. The ocean waves reached 15 feet high, and the wind blew almost 130 miles an hour. The storm killed more than 6,000 people in a few hours. Most of the city was destroyed.

Hurricane Ike Hits Galveston
(*The Daily News*, September 13, 2008)

GALVESTON, Texas. Hurricane Ike hit Galveston and southern parts of the state last night. The storm was not as bad as expected. Still, it destroyed much of the island city.

The city had ordered people to leave the island before the storm. Yet almost half of the people in Galveston stayed. They did not think the storm would be as bad as it was. Winds, floods, and fires have destroyed roads and buildings. The storm has left four people dead so far. Most people still have no power. The flooding has slowed aid to people in most parts of the city.

Directions Have your child read the articles aloud. Ask, "What are two ways the hurricane of 2008 was like that of 1900?" and "What are two ways they were different?" Have your child point to specific parts of the text to support his or her answers.

Name _____

Read the paragraph.

How I Make My Lunch

I like to make my lunch. I make it every morning before
school. First, I make a sandwich. I spread peanut butter on one
piece of bread. I spread honey on another piece of bread. Then
I put the pieces of bread together. I put the sandwich in my lunch
box. Next, I pack an apple or an orange. The last thing I pack is
water. I drink a lot of water! I fill up my water bottle. Then I put it
in my lunch box. I close my lunch box. I take it to school.

Directions Read "How I Make My Lunch" with your child. After you read the paragraph,
ask, "What is the paragraph mostly about?" Then ask, "How do you know?" Finally, ask,
"What are two details from the paragraph?"

Comprehension Lesson 4

Name _____

Read the paragraph.

Fire, the Fish

    I have a pet fish named Fire. Fire is an orange fish with a long tail. His big, round eyes stick out of the sides of his head. Fire likes to swim. Sometimes, if he is afraid, he hides behind the rocks. He lives in a fish tank. I keep Fire in my room. I clean his tank every week. Fire eats fish food. I feed him every day. When he sees the food in the tank, he swims to the top. I take care of him. Fire is a good pet. Maybe I will get another fish. Then Fire will have a friend!

School + Home

Directions Read "Fire, the Fish" with your child. After you read, ask, "What is the paragraph mostly about?" and "How do you know?" Then ask, "What are two details from the paragraph?"

Comprehension Lesson 4 Main Idea and Details **21**

Name _____

Read the article.

All About Bears

There are many kinds of bears. Sun bears are small. Grizzly bears and polar bears are very large. The black bear is common in much of Canada and the United States.

Bears walk on four legs. They can stand up on their back legs. Then they are very tall. Though bears look clumsy, they can run fast. They are also able to climb and swim well. Bears have poor eyesight and hearing. They do most of their hunting by smell. They do not make much sound, but they will growl when they feel afraid or while eating.

Different bears eat different things. Most eat both plants and animals, such as berries, roots, nuts, deer, and fish. Many bears, such as the sun bear, like honey. Polar bears only eat meat. The giant panda only eats bamboo plants.

Bears live in many different habitats. Black bears and grizzly bears live in the forest. Polar bears live in cold, snowy places. Other bears live in warmer places.

Directions Have your child read the article aloud. Ask, "What is the topic of the article?" Then ask, "What is the main idea, or the most important idea about the topic?" and "How do you know?" Finally, ask, "What are three supporting details?"

Comprehension Lesson 4

Read the article.

The Most Popular Ball Game

Soccer is a simple sport that can be played in almost any place. Many people begin playing as young children. In soccer, players can use any part except their hands to move the ball. Our team plays on a field, but people also play soccer in parks, streets, and gyms. When a team gets the ball into the other team's goal, it earns one point. The team with the most points wins.

Cuju, a game much like soccer, was played in China more than 2,400 years ago. Players tried to kick a ball through a hole in a cloth. Modern soccer started in Britain in the 1900s.

Today soccer is the most popular ball sport in the world. More people watch and play soccer than any other ball game. The sport is still popular in Europe and Asia as well as Africa and the Americas.

Directions Have your child read "The Most Popular Ball Game" aloud. Ask, "What is the topic of the article?" Then ask, "What is the main idea, or the most important idea about the topic?" and "How do you know?" Finally, ask, "What are three supporting details?"

Name _____

Read the article.

Destination Hawaii

Every year thousands of people visit Hawaii from all over the world. The warm weather and beautiful views bring people looking to discover new sights as well as those who just want to get away from it all. The state of Hawaii is made up of eight large islands. It also has many smaller islands. Each large island is different from the others.

The island named Hawaii, or the Big Island, was made from five volcanoes. The world's largest volcano is here too. The Big Island also has ocean cliffs, deserts, thick forests, and snow-covered mountains. The island of Oahu has the most people, shops, and places to eat. The capital city is also here. Oahu has some of the best beaches in the world. The island of Lanai was once important for growing pineapples. On Kauai is a large canyon. It is about 3,500 feet deep and ten miles long. A mountain on Kauai is known as the wettest place on Earth. The mountain gets about 450 inches of rain each year!

These are just a few of the islands and their sights. Come see for yourself what Hawaii has to offer!

Directions Have your child read "Destination Hawaii" aloud. Ask, "What is the topic of the article?" Then ask, "What is the main idea of the article?" Finally, ask, "What are three supporting details?" Have your child check that the main idea is supported by the details from the article.

Comprehension Lesson 4

Read the article.

The Dust Bowl

One of the worst droughts in history hit the Great Plains in the 1930s. By that time a drop in crop prices and changes in farming were already hurting farmers. Once the drought came, families saw their life's work dry up almost overnight. More than two million people in Oklahoma, Kansas, and other Great Plains states had to move.

After World War I, the price of farm crops dropped. Farmers needed to grow more crops to make up for the low prices. They bought costly farm tools. They started using the land for growing wheat instead of for raising cattle. Many farmers went into debt.

In 1931, a drought came and lasted for seven years. The soil was weak from too much farming. Spring winds blew away the soil. The blowing soil caused black dust storms. These gave the Dust Bowl its name.

Many farmers lost everything. They packed up their things and headed for California and its sunny weather. Its long growing season seemed to promise a better life. By the 1940s, the drought had ended. Yet by then, many farmers had already started new lives.

Directions Have your child read "The Dust Bowl" aloud. Ask, "What is the topic of the article?" Then ask, "What is the main idea of the article?" Finally, ask, "What are three supporting details?" Have your child check that the main idea is supported by the details from the article.

Name _____

Read the story.

In the Leaves

One day in fall, I was playing outside. I wanted to jump in a pile of leaves. Then I saw the pile start to move! I did not know what was happening. I was a little scared. I did not know what was in there.

Next, my dad walked over to the leaves. He bent down. Then he moved some of the leaves. At last, a squirrel ran out! It ran under a fence. Then it ran up a tree. Now I know I am not the only one who plays in the leaves!

School + Home **Directions** Read "In the Leaves" together with your child. Ask your child, "What happens first?" "What happens next?" and "What happens after that?"

Comprehension Lesson 5

Name _____

Read the paragraph.

My Own Snowflakes

In winter, I make my own snow. I hang it in the windows. First, I cover the table with a cloth. The cloth protects the table. Then I get out a square piece of paper. I fold it in half to make a triangle. Then I fold it again. Then I fold it into three parts and cut the bottom. Next, I cut shapes out of the paper. Any shapes will work. After that, I open the paper. Then I rub it flat. There are tiny holes where I cut the paper. When I finish, I hang the beautiful snowflakes in our windows! Each snowflake is different!

 Directions Read "My Own Snowflakes" together with your child, paying attention to the order of the steps. Ask, "What step is first?" "What step is next?" and "What step is last?" Then have your child tell the steps in the correct sequence in his or her own words.

Name _____

Read the story.

Flash's First Race

Last summer my brother gave me a turtle for my birthday. He had named him Flash as a joke because turtles are so slow. A lot of the other kids in my neighborhood have turtles as pets too. Last Saturday we had a turtle race in a sandbox at the park. I entered Flash in the race.

That morning four other turtles were entered in the race. At noon the race started. First, the turtles were off to a slow start. Then Jessie's turtle climbed out of the box, so he lost. It was a hot day, so I sprayed water on Flash as he walked. Then the other kids started spraying their turtles with water too. Soon the sand was all wet, and the turtles were walking even slower than usual. After about 20 minutes Flash crossed the finish line first! At last the race was over, and Flash won.

Directions Have your child read "Flash's First Race" aloud. Ask your child to circle all the sequence clue words. Then ask, "What happened?" Have your child retell the story in the correct sequence.

Comprehension Lesson 5

Name _____

Read the article.

Owen and Mzee

Owen is a baby hippopotamus. Mzee is a large, 130-year-old tortoise. They are very different animals, but they have a special friendship.

In 2004, Owen lost his parents because of a bad storm. After the storm was over, some villagers found him alone on a reef. They used ropes and nets, as well as boats and cars, to rescue him. Once they rescued him, they took him to a special wildlife park.

The hippo was tired and scared when he got to the park. The park rangers put Owen in Mzee's large pen. Owen ran to the tortoise immediately, as if he were Owen's mother. At first, Mzee would ignore Owen. But very soon, Mzee started to share his food and play with Owen. He even follows him on walks sometimes. Now they are good friends.

Directions Have your child read "Owen and Mzee" aloud. Ask your child to picture the events in his or her mind while reading. Remind your child that not all selections have clue words. Then have your child tell what events happened first, next, and last.

Comprehension Lesson 5

Name _____

Read the article.

How Crayons Are Made

Crayons are fun to use. Children use them all the time at home and at school. Each one is made the same way.

All crayons are made of wax. First, a machine heats up the wax, which is stored in a large tank. Then color is added. The color mixes with the wax. The colored wax is heated until it melts. After that, the wax gets poured into molds. Each mold is full of holes that are shaped like crayons. After the wax is poured, water is added for cooling. During cooling, the wax cools off, and the crayons get hard. People check to make sure the crayons are not broken. They take out any that are broken or damaged. The damaged pieces will be melted down and used again.

Then a machine wraps paper around each crayon. Each color has a name. A machine places the crayons in boxes. Each box goes into a truck, and off they go to stores. At last, some end up at your house!

Directions Have your child read "How Crayons Are Made" aloud. Ask your child to picture the events in his or her mind while reading. Ask, "Which events happen simultaneously, or at the same time?" and "How do you know?" Then have your child tell the events in his or her own words in the correct sequence.

Comprehension Lesson 5

Name _____

Read the article.

Angel of the Battlefield

When war broke out in 1861, the army was not well prepared to help the wounded. To fix that, Clara Barton tried to bring her own supplies to the fields to help hurt soldiers. However, the army refused. Finally, Barton was allowed to help.

In 1862, Barton brought a wagon full of bandages to the fields. While bullets flew past, she brought water and food to sick soldiers. She nursed their wounds and helped the doctors. Once, as Barton bent down to give a man some water, she felt her sleeve shake. Then she saw that a bullet had torn through her dress. It had killed the man she was helping. Barton moved on, helping others who needed her.

Barton was able to stay strong and help others, even when her own life was in danger. Yet she had been a very shy child. Her parents worried about her. At age sixteen, she became a teacher to cure her shy ways. During her teaching, she set up a free public school. Then the school hired a male in her place. Barton then left to help with the war. She helped thousands of men through some of the worst battles of the war.

Directions Have your child read "Angel of the Battlefield" aloud. Ask your child to picture the events in his or her mind while reading. Ask, "Which events are told out of order?" and "How do you know?" Then have your child tell the events in his or her own words in the correct sequence.

Name _____

Read the story.

Spring Tryouts

Jen had seen her friend Laura in a school play. It looked like fun! Jen decided to try out for the spring play. She practiced her lines by herself. Then she practiced in front of Laura. Laura helped her read the words with feeling.

At last, the day came. The room was silent. Jen took a deep breath. Her hands were wet. Yet she read her lines with feeling.

The next day, there was a list in the hall of those who made it. Jen looked for her name. Then she pointed, gasped, and hugged Laura.

Directions Read "Spring Tryouts" with your child. Then ask, "Do you think Jen got the part in the play?" and "How can you tell?" Have your child support his or her conclusion with details from the story and his or her own experience.

Comprehension Lesson 6

Name _____

Read the story.

The Mess

Billy left his clothes in the hall and his toys on the floor. His parents always told him to pick up his things.

That summer, Billy's friend Pat got a new puppy. Pat asked Billy to spend the night. Yet Billy's parents were worried. "You will have to pick up your things," said Billy's father. Billy said he would.

Billy went to Pat's house. He threw his bag on the floor. He petted Pat's puppy. Then he ran outside to play. He forgot about his bag. Later that night, Billy and Pat came home. Billy's clothes were all over the house!

Directions Read "The Mess" with your child. Then ask, "What do you think happened to Billy's clothes?" and "How can you tell?" Have your child support his or her conclusion with details from the story and his or her own experience.

Comprehension Lesson 6

Draw Conclusions **33**

Name _____

Read the story.

Late Again!

Josh is always late. He does not try to be late, but he just cannot get to places on time. His brother Matt is tired of Josh being late.

One day Josh and Matt saw an ad in the paper for free tickets for a new movie. "First come, first served!" said the ad. "Come to the theater after school tomorrow." Josh and Matt were excited. They had both wanted to see that movie. They decided to meet after school and get the tickets together.

On the next day, Matt waited for his brother outside. Josh hurried, but his locker got stuck. Then he could not find his math book. At last, he met his brother outside. Matt's face was red. "Don't you know what time it is?" he said through his teeth. Then he grabbed Josh's arm and started running.

Directions Have your child read "Late Again!" aloud. Then ask, "How does Matt feel when he sees Josh outside?" "Why?" and "How can you tell?" Have your child support his or her conclusion with details from the story.

Comprehension Lesson 6

Read the article.

The Homestead Act

In 1862, President Lincoln signed the Homestead Act. The act gave away free public land in the Great Plains. To receive the land, the settlers had to pay a small filing fee and agree to live on the land for at least five years.

The promise of free land brought many people out west. Yet settling the land was not easy. The journey out west was difficult. Many people left their friends and families behind. Starting a successful farm took hard work and a lot of luck. Sometimes weather or insects destroyed the crops. At first, there were few other people, so settlers had to learn to do everything on their own.

By 1900, 600,000 homestead claims were filed. Trains made travel easier. More and more people moved west. The Homestead Act was a success.

Directions Have your child read "The Homestead Act" aloud. Then ask, "Why do you think the government wanted to give free land to settlers?" and "How can you tell?" Have your child support his or her conclusion with details from the article.

Name _____

Read the article.

Town Shocked by Walking Catfish

PINELLAS PARK, Florida—People in a south Florida town saw a shocking sight yesterday. "Fish were walking across the street!" said Dave Brown. Brown was driving when he saw several fish in the street. Due to heavy rains, the street drains had flooded. Large catfish were in the flooded parts of the street, walking around in the low water. "It was wild," said Brown. "We thought for sure it was some kind of joke. There were fish all over!"

Yet, the fish were no joke. Kate Rivers, a Florida scientist, explained the strange sight. Walking catfish have an organ like a lung to breathe air. They often live in ponds, ditches, and storm drains. When drains flood, the fish end up on the street. As long as they stay wet, they can use their fins to "walk" on land.

In the 1960s, the catfish were brought from Asia, and some got loose in Florida. After ten years, walking catfish had spread across the southern part of the state. The fish often eat the eggs of other local fish. Now they are well known as a pest.

Directions Have your child read "Town Shocked by Walking Catfish" aloud. Then ask, "How do you think walking catfish were able to spread across Florida so quickly?" Say, "Draw conclusions based on the article."

Read the story.

The Cut

When Amy got home from school, her mother told her to watch her little sister Tina. Amy's mother had to pick up the family's clothes from the cleaners. Amy's family was going to Uncle Jack's wedding that weekend.

Amy helped Tina make a wedding gift for Uncle Jack. First, Tina drew pictures of flowers and colored them. Amy helped Tina cut out each flower. "Don't cut too much," said Amy. Tina loved using scissors and would probably cut the flowers into tiny pieces if she could, thought Amy.

Just then, Amy heard the door slam. Her mother was home. "Amy!" called her mother. "Come help me carry the stuff in from the car!" Amy ran out to help.

"We had better check on your sister," Amy's mother said after they had moved everything from the car inside. Amy went to Tina's room. The colored flowers were on Tina's bed. The scissors were not there. Amy could hear Tina in the bathroom. She opened the door and saw the floor covered with bits of blond.

"That's not paper," thought Amy nervously, afraid to look at her sister.

Directions Have your child read "The Cut" aloud. Then ask, "What do you think Tina is doing in the bathroom?" and "What details from the story help you draw that conclusion?" Then ask, "Why do you think the conclusion that Tina was cutting more paper flowers in the bathroom is probably not valid?"

Read the story.

The Watch

Kate and Pete's father wanted to get their mother a watch. It was her birthday. "I need you two to help me out," he said. He always had a hard time picking out gifts.

At the store, Pete pointed to a blue watch. "She'd love this one," he said. Their father looked at it.

Kate rolled her eyes. "Pete, you just like that one because you like blue," said Kate. "Mom likes red best."

"But everything she has is red," said Pete.

"Pete's got a point," said their father. He scratched his head. "How about we call and ask her?"

Kate and Pete nodded.

Directions Read "The Watch" with your child. Ask, "Who are the characters in the story?" Then have your child describe what each character says, thinks, and does. Finally, ask, "Are the characters realistic or make-believe?" and "How can you tell?"

Comprehension Lesson 7

Read the story.

Raccoon's Neighbor

Fox moved next door to Raccoon. At first, Raccoon was happy. Fox was a kind neighbor. Fox brought Raccoon fresh cream pies each week. He often stopped by Raccoon's place just to chat. Then he started to ignore Raccoon. He stopped bringing pies, and he stopped visiting.

"Well!" cried Raccoon. He missed the cream pies, and he could not stand being ignored.

At last, Raccoon called Fox. He wanted to give him a piece of his mind, but Fox spoke first. "I am so glad you called!" he said. "I have been sick all month. It's so good to hear from a friend!"

"Yes," said Raccoon. "It is!"

School + Home

Directions Read "Raccoon's Neighbor" together with your child. Ask, "Who are the characters in the story?" Then have your child describe what each character says, thinks, and does. Finally, ask, "Are the characters realistic or make-believe?" and "How can you tell?"

Name _____

Read the story.

Mr. Field's Dogs

Chris is young and strong, and he is almost as tall as his neighbor, Mr. Field. After school, Chris helps Mr. Field with his dogs. Mr. Field has thin, white hair and a warm smile. He walks slowly around the yard with his cane. He uses his cane to point out things to Chris. "See that robin in the tree, son? She's building a nest up there," said Mr. Field. "Poor thing. The dogs keep chasing her."

Each afternoon, Chris helps Mr. Field feed his dogs. Then Chris takes the dogs for a walk. He loves to run around the yard with them until they are tired. Mr. Field watches from his lawn chair, laughing.

"Mr. Field, I'm beat!" Chris said when he finished. He smiled at the dogs lying on their backs, and he wiped his forehead.

"You and them both!" said Mr. Field, scratching his dogs behind their ears.

Directions Have your child read "Mr. Field's Dogs" aloud. Ask your child to describe Chris and Mr. Field, describing what each character looks like, says, thinks, and does. Then ask, "How do you think Mr. Field feels when Chris plays with his dogs?" Have your child use details from the story to support his or her answer.

40 Character

Comprehension Lesson 7

Name _____

Read the story.

Under the Stars

"Tonight's the night!" thought Rachel, smiling. She had invited her best friend Joy to spend the night. Both girls had long hair they wore in ponytails. They would be in sixth grade next fall. Rachel's father pitched a tent in the backyard so Rachel and Joy could sleep under the stars. "Please don't let Julie bother us," said Rachel. Rachel's little sister Julie always got into everything. Rachel knew she would try and ruin the night.

"Don't worry. Julie is staying at your grandmother's," said Rachel's mother. Rachel breathed a sigh of relief.

That night Rachel got everything ready for camping in the backyard. Julie danced in the tent, played with the flashlight, and messed up the snacks, but Rachel didn't say a thing.

At last Joy came over. Rachel's mother was getting Julie ready to go to her grandmother's when the phone rang. It was her grandmother. Rachel shot Joy a nervous look. "Oh, no," she whispered.

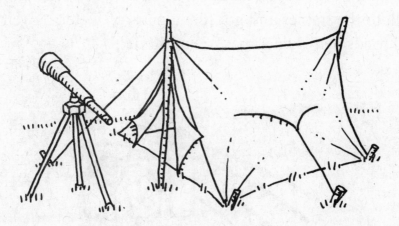

Directions Have your child read "Under the Stars" aloud. Ask your child to describe what each character looks like, says, thinks, and does. Then ask, "How do you think Rachel feels when Julie plays in the tent?" "How does Rachel feel when the phone rings?" and "How do you know?"

Read the story.

Heatstroke

Dan squinted in the sun. It was only 9 a.m., but the air was hot and thick. Tony was talking, but Dan tuned out his cousin in the heat.

"Dan? Hello? Hello in there!" Tony was thirteen, but he was shorter than Dan. His face was red, especially when he was angry, which happened often. Dan was only eleven, so their uncle left Tony in charge of the ranch. Tony took it seriously.

"So, Dan, you can clean the stables. I will ride the horses to keep them loose. Deal?" It was just like Tony to make Dan do all the work, but Dan kept quiet. "There's nothing a hothead like Tony likes better than picking a fight," Dan's dad had warned. Dan was angry but walked to the stables in silence.

After half an hour, Dan heard a thud. He saw Tony passed out on the grass. The heat! "Serves him right," thought Dan at first. He called, but Tony did not answer. He called again. Then Dan's breath caught in his throat, and he threw down his rake, running as fast as he could toward his cousin.

As soon as Dan reached Tony, he opened his eyes. Dan helped him walk to the stables and got him a glass of water. "Even a hothead needs help sometimes," Dan thought.

Directions Have your child read "Heatstroke" aloud. Ask your child to describe what Dan and Tony look like, say, think, and do. Then ask, "How do you learn about Tony through other characters' dialogue, thoughts, and actions?" "How does Dan change in the story?" and "Why does he change?"

Read the story.

Fresh Flowers

Mary heard someone scraping around in the garden next door. She pulled the curtain back to look. "Get a load of this, Fred," she told her husband. "Fran is playing in the dirt again." Fred looked up from his paper but did not say anything. "Her nails are black as coal. Then she picks up her grandchildren with those hands!" Mary looked at her own hands. Her nails were clean and long and painted a rosy pink.

Fred cracked his newspaper. "Oh, she's not hurting anyone."

"Not yet," said Mary. "Not until she spreads some disease."

Fred laughed. "Hey, I heard she found a snake out there last week." Mary shuddered in disgust. "Good for her."

The next week, Mary was having a dinner party and wanted fresh flowers for the table. It looked like Fran wasn't home. Fran had so many flowers, and some grew into Mary's yard. Mary would just cut a few stems.

As Mary stepped outside, Fran stood up. Mary had not seen her picking weeds. "Oh!" cried Mary, dropping her scissors.

"Feel free to cut some of my roses," said Fran. "I don't mind. But watch where you step. I think you have a family of garter snakes under your porch."

Directions Have your child read "Fresh Flowers" aloud. Ask your child to describe Mary and Fran based on what they look like, say, think, do, and what others say and think about them. Then ask, "How do you learn about Fran through other characters' dialogue, thoughts, and actions?" "How do you learn about Mary?" and "How does Mary change in the story?"

Read the story.

Saturday's Party

Sam's birthday is next week. He wanted to have a big party on Saturday. He would invite all his friends. His mother said she would make a cake. His brother said he would plan games for the party.

Then he went to school today. His friend Jose invited him to *his* birthday party on Saturday.

At first Sam was disappointed. He told Jose about his own party plans. Then he had an idea. "Jose, let's have one big party with all our friends!"

"Great idea!" said Jose.

Directions Read "Saturday's Party" with your child. Ask, "What is the problem in the story?" and "What is the solution?" Then ask your child to say what happened at the beginning, middle, and end of the story.

Read the story.

The Parade

Josh was disappointed. He was supposed to play his horn in the town parade. Then last week he broke his leg. Now he could not walk. In his town, playing in the parade was a big deal. Josh had always wanted to be a part of it.

The day of the parade came. Josh sat looking out the window. All of a sudden, his friend Ben ran up to his door. He was pushing a wheelchair.

"Hop in!" said Ben. "I can push you while you play."

"Thanks!" Josh said. He was happy to have such a good friend.

Directions Read "The Parade" with your child. Ask, "What is the problem in the story?" and "What is the solution?" Then have your child tell you what happens at the beginning, middle, and end of the story.

Name _____

Read the story.

Tornado in Lake County

Ed and his wife bought a small farm. It had been Ed's dream to be a farmer.

Then, on one spring day, Ed saw storm clouds rolling in. The air became thick and still, and the sky looked green. The radio issued a tornado warning for Lake County, where Ed and his wife lived.

Ed rushed his cows inside the barn. His wife closed all the windows in the house. Then Ed saw the funnel cloud spinning toward his fields. He stopped for a moment to watch it. He was angry. He had worked so hard, and now his farm would be destroyed. Finally, his wife called him, and Ed went to the basement with her.

At last, the storm stopped. Ed went outside to check the damage. He and his wife were fine. His cows were afraid, but they were not hurt. The fields were torn up, and the barn had lost its roof, but those things could be fixed. Ed was relieved. He was eager to start repairs.

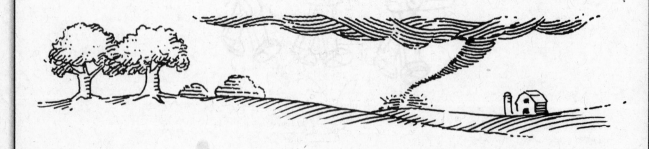

Directions Have your child read "Tornado in Lake County" aloud. Ask, "What is the problem in the story?" and "What is the solution?" Then have your child list the important events of the story in order.

46 Plot

Comprehension Lesson 8

Name _____

Read the story.

Keeping Pip

    Mrs. Potter was the oldest person on Willow Street. She had a small dog named Pip. Pip was still a young dog and had a lot of energy.

    One day Mrs. Potter told her neighbor Mr. Davis that she had to find another home for Pip. She loved him very much, but she had a bad hip, and she was too tired to take him on long walks every day. She was very sad to give up her dog.

    . Mr. Davis felt bad for Mrs. Potter. He talked to the other neighbors. The next day he said, "Mrs. Potter, you don't have to give Pip away. Everyone on the street is going to take turns walking him for you!"

    "Oh! Thank you!" Mrs. Potter said. "I'm so happy, and I know Pip will be happy too."

Directions Have your child read "Keeping Pip" aloud. Ask, "What is the problem in the story?" and "What is the solution?" Then have your child list the important events of the story in order.

Comprehension Lesson 8

Plot **47**

Name _____

Read the story.

The Accident

Laurie walked into the office holding onto her mother's hand. She had tears in her eyes, and her breath caught in her throat. The cut on her arm was very sore and bright red. Her mother had cleaned the cut and put bandages on it, but she did not know if it was infected. Laurie worried that her doctor would tell her she needed to go to the hospital.

Laurie's mother was also worried. Her daughter had been helping rake leaves out in the garden. She had cut her arm when she tripped on a garden rake. The metal rake was dirty, and the cut looked serious. Laurie tried to relax and read a magazine in the waiting room, but she feared the worst.

The doctor finally saw Laurie and her mother. To everyone's relief, she told them that Laurie would not need to go to the hospital. The doctor cleaned the cut and put a new bandage on it. Then she gave Laurie a shot. She said the shot would keep her from getting sick from the rusty rake.

On the way home, Laurie's mother hugged her daughter. "No more yard work for you for a while!" she said.

Directions Have your child read "The Accident" aloud. Ask, "What is the conflict in the story?" and "What events build the conflict?" Then have your child tell you how the conflict is resolved.

Read the story.

Snow Concert

Lila was excited when she woke up in the morning. Today she would be singing in her first school concert. Her class had practiced all year for it.

When she got dressed and came downstairs, she knew something was wrong. The windows were coated with slushy ice. A blanket of white covered the yard and street. It had snowed a foot overnight! And freezing rain started coming down. It was a mess! Her mother told her school was closed today because of the weather. She thought Lila would be happy about the snow day.

"But what about my concert?" Lila cried.

"I am sure you can give it on another day," her mother said. Still, Lila was upset. She had been looking forward to singing *today.* Her mother did not understand at all. The snow had ruined everything.

Later that morning, the doorbell rang. Lila's friends were at the door. They said they were going to walk to a nearby Senior Center and sing for the people there. They asked if she'd like to join them.

"What a great idea!" Lila said. She ran to get her coat and snow boots.

Directions Have your child read "Snow Concert" aloud. Ask, "What is the conflict in the story?" and "Who or what is the conflict between?" Then ask, "What events build the conflict?" Finally, have your child tell you how the conflict is resolved.

Name _____

Read the play.

Juan's Birthday

(Cast: Juan, Val, Mom)
(Setting: outside a house)
(Curtain opens. Juan is sitting on a porch, holding his head in his hands and looking sad. Val walks up to the porch. She is hiding a wrapped gift behind her back.)
VAL: What's wrong, Juan?
JUAN: Today is my birthday, but no one remembered, not even my mom.
VAL: That's too bad. Can we go in your house? I'd like a glass of water, please.
(Juan opens the door. Mom is standing there.)
MOM: Juan. I'm so glad you came inside for your party. All your friends have been waiting!
(From inside the house, many voices call, "Surprise!")
JUAN: They didn't forget!

Directions Read "Juan's Birthday" with your child. Ask, "When does this story take place?" and "Where does it take place?" Have your child be as specific as possible. Then ask, "Could the setting be real, or is it imaginary?" and "How do you know?"

Comprehension Lesson 9

Read the article.

The Great Chicago Fire

In 1871, many people lived in Chicago. More people moved in every year. At that time, most homes were made out of wood.

The city saw little rain in 1871. That fall a fire started in a barn. The city's dry weather and wind helped the fire spread fast. In minutes, wood homes went up in smoke. Even stone and brick homes burned to the ground. The fire grew, burning down block after block. It continued for two days. It spread over three miles. Soon the fire burned down much of the city.

At last it rained. People put the fire out. Yet many people had lost their homes. Hundreds of people died.

School + Home

Directions Read "The Great Chicago Fire" with your child. Ask, "What is the setting (time and place) of the article?" Then ask, "Is the setting real or imaginary?" and "How do you know?"

Name _____

Read the story.

Hansel and Gretel

Long ago, there lived two children named Hansel and Gretel. Their father told them to play by the house and to stay away from the woods where they might get lost. One day, the children grew curious. They wandered near the tall trees behind their house. They walked and walked. Soon they became hungry, but they could not find their way home. They saw only trees. Suddenly, they found a large house made of cookies and candy.

Hansel and Gretel started eating the house. Just then, an old lady opened the door and caught them. "My house!" she cried. "Now you will get what you deserve!" She grabbed the children with her large, crooked hands. She carried them toward her blazing oven. But when she opened the oven to put the children in, they escaped!

Hansel and Gretel then ran and ran until they found their way back home.

School + Home

Directions Have your child read "Hansel and Gretel" aloud. Ask your child, "Where and when does the story take place?" and "What details help you figure out the setting?" Then have your child tell whether the setting is real or imaginary and how he or she can tell.

Read the story.

Father's Day

Grandfather walked down the long driveway and opened his mailbox. The metal box had grown hot in the summer sun. He picked a stack of bills out of the box. "Bills and more bills!" thought Grandfather. Then he noticed a red envelope. It was from Jeff, his grandson.

Grandfather had almost forgotten. Next Sunday was Father's Day! Jeff would be spending a week with him to celebrate. Grandfather had been so busy working around the house that he hadn't planned anything yet for Jeff's visit.

Grandfather brought the mail inside. He got a drink of water and sat down to rest. He started making a list. They could go swimming in the lake and fishing off the pier. They could go hiking in the woods. Jeff was a city kid, but Grandfather knew he would have fun in the country too.

Directions Have your child read aloud "Father's Day." Ask your child, "Where and when does the story take place?" and "What details in the story helped you figure out the setting?" Have your child circle details in the story that helped him or her infer the setting.

Name _____

Read the story.

Saturday on Ice

Jim grabbed his skates from the shelf in the basement. It had been ages since he had been ice-skating! He couldn't wait.

Upstairs, Jim's friend Van was waiting. Jim rushed to put on his coat, hat, gloves, and boots. Then each boy hung his skates over his shoulder. "Jim, be home by five," yelled his mother.

"Okay!" Then Jim looked at Van. Jim did not have a watch, and neither did Van. Jim saw his father's watch sitting on the counter. He never wore a watch on weekends. He would not miss it today. Jim put it in his pocket.

Jim and Van got to the lake and shoveled off a place for skating. They played hockey until the sun started to set. Jim pulled down his glove to check the time, but the watch was gone! Jim and Van looked everywhere. At last they decided to go home without it.

At home, Jim told his parents what happened. He did not even have his coat off yet. He looked at the floor and put his hands in his pockets. He knew he was in trouble. Just then he felt something heavy in his pocket—the watch!

Directions Have your child read aloud "Saturday on Ice." Ask, "What is the setting?" and "How does it affect the action in the story?" Then ask, "How does the setting affect Jim's character in the story?" Finally, have your child tell how the story might be different if it took place in a different setting.

tting

Name _____

Read the story.

The Attic

Jane stayed with her Aunt Sue while her parents went on a trip. Aunt Sue had a large garden that Jane loved to play in. When she visited, Jane often helped with the planting and weeding. She would help Aunt Sue pick vegetables for dinner and bake fruit pies for dessert.

Yet this visit was different. It was late in the year, and the vegetables had been picked. The fruit and flowers were gone. The garden was dry and dead. Jane wondered what she would do.

"Well," said Aunt Sue, joking, "You could help me clean the attic!" Aunt Sue was then going to suggest they go see a movie instead, but Jane interrupted.

"You have an attic? Can I see it?"

"Seriously?" asked Aunt Sue. "Well, sure." She took Jane up to the attic. It was filled to the ceiling with boxes and furniture. They found Aunt Sue's high school yearbook. Then they found Uncle Ron's records and some toys that were even older than Aunt Sue. Jane laughed at old pictures of her parents.

Aunt Sue told Jane the story behind each item. After the visit, Jane felt like she had seen a side of her family she had never known before.

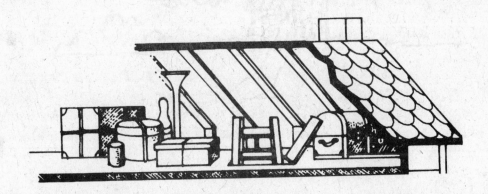

Directions Have your child read aloud "The Attic." Ask, "What is the setting?" and "How does it affect the action in the story?" Then ask, "How does the setting affect Jane in the story?" Finally, have your child tell how the story might be different if it took place outdoors in summer.

Name _____

Read the story.

A Little Help

Mouse was very hungry. He saw a big, red apple high in a tree. Mouse was very small. He could not reach the apple in the tree.

Turtle, Rabbit, and Fox came by. Mouse said, "I would like that apple. Will you please help me?"

"Sure!" they said.

Turtle stood under the tree. Fox stood on top of Turtle. Rabbit stood on top of Fox. Then Mouse stood on Rabbit's head. With the help of his friends, Mouse was able to reach up and pick the apple.

It was delicious!

Directions Read "A Little Help" with your child. Ask, "What happens in the beginning, middle, and end of the story?" and "What does Mouse learn?" Then have your child say what he or she thinks is the big idea or meaning of the story.

ne

Name _____

Read the story.

Not Goodbye

May was very sad. Summer camp was almost over. May had to leave her new best friends, Jen, Ann, and Kathy. They all lived far away from each other. They might not see each other until next summer. May thought it would be a sad year without her friends.

"I know what we can do," said Jen. "Let's promise to e-mail each other every week."

"We can send pictures too!" said Kathy, who loved taking pictures.

The last day of camp came. Yet the girls did not feel so sad. They knew that they could still keep in touch.

School + Home

Directions Read "Not Goodbye" with your child. Ask, "What happens in the beginning, middle, and end of the story?" and "What does May learn?" Then have your child say what he or she thinks is the big idea or meaning of the story.

Comprehension Lesson 10

Theme **57**

Name _____

Read the story.

The Hare and the Tortoise

"I have never lost a race!" Hare bragged to the other animals. "I challenge anyone here to try to beat me!"

The animals were silent. At last Tortoise said softly, "I will race."

Hare had a good laugh at this. "You?" he asked pointing. "But I could run circles around you!"

"Do not boast until after the race," said Tortoise.

The animals prepared the course. When the race started, Hare ran quickly out of sight. Yet he was not worried about Tortoise, so he decided to take a short nap.

In the meantime, slow Tortoise walked and walked toward the finish line. At last he passed Hare, who was still asleep. By the time Hare woke up, Tortoise was almost to the finish line. Hare jumped up and ran as fast as he could, but he could not beat Tortoise to the finish line. After Tortoise finished, he told Hare, "Slow and steady wins the race."

Directions Have your child read "The Hare and the Tortoise" aloud. Ask, "What does Hare learn in the story?" "What is the theme?" and "Is the theme stated directly in the story?"

Comprehension Lesson 10

Name _____

Read the story.

The Clothes That Were Invited to Dinner

Marco was a poor boy who lived long ago. He was a good boy, but no one in his village was kind to him. No one spoke nicely to him or gave him anything to eat. Once Marco went to a farmhouse and asked for food. The farmer saw how ragged Marco looked and had his guard dogs chase Marco away.

When Marco's grandmother heard how Marco was treated, she sewed a fine coat, a pair of pants, and a velvet vest for him to wear.

Marco dressed in his new clothes and went to the same farm. The farmer now made a great fuss! He invited Marco to dinner. He paid him great respect during the meal. Marco, with one hand, filled his stomach. With his other hand, he put the food that was left over into his pockets, saying: "Eat, my clothes, for *you* were invited!" Marco's grandmother had told him that many people care more about how a person looks than what a person is like.

School + Home

Directions Have your child read "The Clothes That Were Invited to Dinner" aloud. Ask, "What does Marco learn in the story?" "What is the theme?" and "What evidence in the text supports this theme?"

Name _____

Read the story.

Trouble at the Table

Dinner was ready. Victor's mother asked him to set the table. Victor sighed. "Why can't Sara set the table?" he asked.

"Because I asked you," said his mother. Victor then set the table for his mother, his sister Sara, and himself. His mother brought dinner to the table.

Sara also hated to set the table. She was glad Victor had to do it instead of her. Sara ran into the room and put her napkin on her head. Her mother raised her eyebrows. Victor rolled his eyes. Sara put her napkin on her lap.

Their mother put salad on the plates. Sara used a spoon to pick up the salad. Most of the lettuce fell off the spoon.

"Why don't you use your fork like we do?" Victor asked.

"I am special. I didn't have to set the table," Sara told him.

Sara cut her macaroni and cheese with a knife. Her mother said, "Sara, you know better than that." Then Sara tried to eat her pudding with a fork.

Finally, their mother had had enough. "Sara," she said, "tomorrow night *you* will set the table." Sara sighed. Victor smiled. Their mother just shook her head.

Directions Have your child read "Trouble at the Table" aloud. Ask, "What is one theme in the story?" "Is it stated or implied?" and "What details from the text support this theme?"

Comprehension Lesson 10

Name _____

Read the stories.

Skip

Dan and Carlos always walked their dogs together. Dan's dog, Red, was a puppy. Carlos's dog, Skip, was much older. Skip was slow, but he loved walking with the others.

One day Dan knocked on Carlos's door, but no one was home. The next week Carlos said that Skip had gotten sick and died. Carlos didn't want to go for walks. He was too sad about Skip.

Dan's mother said to give Carlos some time. A few weeks later, Dan knocked on Carlos's door. "I thought it might be fun if we went for a walk again," he said. "Red misses you too."

"Okay," said Carlos. "I think I'm ready." He still missed Skip, but the walk reminded him of the fun they had had together.

The Oak Tree

After the storm, Al and his father walked around the yard. The strong winds had knocked down the fence, and rain had flooded the grass.

"Oh, no," said his father, pointing. "Look."

A large oak tree stood in the middle of the yard. Now the tree was split down the middle. Al helped his father pull off the broken branches. He worried that the tree would have to be cut down, but his father left it alone.

Later in the season, the tree looked better. Some new shoots had even started growing. "I think this tree will make it," said Al's father. "It just takes some time to heal, that's all."

School + Home

Directions Have your child read "Skip" and "The Oak Tree" aloud. Ask, "What is one theme in 'Skip'?" "What is one theme in the 'The Oak Tree'?" and "What theme do both stories share?" Have your child support responses with evidence from the text.

Comprehension Lesson 10

Name _____

Read the story.

My Uncle, the Firefighter

Uncle Rob is a brave firefighter. He works hard to put out fires in our town. He puts out brush fires. He also puts out house fires. He helps people get out of burning cars. He saves people.

One morning, Uncle Rob took me to the fire station. Uncle Rob works with a man named Jack. Jack also fights fires. He told me a story. "Your uncle is very brave," Jack said. "He went into a burning house. He helped the people get out." I was very proud of Uncle Rob when I heard this story about him.

Uncle Rob is good at his job. He always tries to help other people.

Directions Read "My Uncle, the Firefighter" together with your child. Have your child retell the most important events in order by telling the character's goals, how he tried to reach those goals, and whether or not he accomplished them.

Name _____

Read the article.

New York City

Have you ever been to New York City? It has many things to see and do. It is also the largest city in the country. In New York City, you can visit the Empire State Building. It is 102 stories tall! You can also visit the Statue of Liberty. It is over 300 feet tall. People come from all over the world to see it. Another place to visit is Central Park. It is a big park with many lakes. People like to play and rest in this park. New York City has something for all.

Directions Have your child read "New York City" aloud. Help your child identify the main ideas and important details in the article. Then have your child summarize the article using his or her own words.

Comprehension Lesson 11

Retell/Summarize **63**

Name _____

Read the story.

A Great Chef

Betty loved to cook. She was always in the kitchen watching her parents cook. Her father could work magic in the kitchen.

One day, Betty told her father, "I want to be a great chef someday." Her father was very happy. He said, "That's a fabulous idea, but it will take a lot of hard work." He told Betty she would have to practice cooking many different kinds of food.

After that, Betty cooked every day. After school, she chopped and diced vegetables. She became very good at cutting them all the same size. She made all kinds of different foods. Her family tried out all of Betty's creations, and they told her which meals tasted best. They constantly encouraged her. They said, "Your food is delicious! You will be a great chef."

Today Betty owns *Betty's Place*. It's the best restaurant in town!

Directions Have your child read "A Great Chef" aloud. Have your child retell the most important events in order by telling the character's goals, how she tried to reach those goals, and whether or not she accomplished them.

Comprehension Lesson 11

Name _____

Read the article.

Siberian Dwarf Hamsters

Dwarf hamsters are interesting pets. They are only about 4 inches long. They have short heads and very small ears. Originally, they came from northern Russia. Their fur is dark gray. In the winter, hamsters living in the wild grow a white coat to match the color of the snow. Their coats change because they are sensitive to the sun's light. This change helps protect them from other animals. Dwarf hamsters that are kept inside as pets are not always able to sense changes in sunlight. Pet hamsters often do not change color.

Dwarf hamsters eat fruits, vegetables, and seeds. They like to peel and shred food. Pet owners can place whole apples, peas, and melons in the cage for the hamsters to peel and eat.

A dwarf hamster can live alone or share a cage with another dwarf hamster. If the hamsters get upset, they make noise. Dwarf hamsters seldom fight. They are friendly and loveable.

Directions Have your child read "Siberian Dwarf Hamsters" aloud. Ask your child to underline the most important ideas in the article. Then have him or her summarize the article.

Name _____

Read the story.

Sick Day

Victor woke up this morning feeling horrible. He tried to shout for his mother, but his voice cracked.

"Did you say something, Victor?" Mom asked.

"Mom, I feel really sick. My nose is all runny, and everything hurts. My throat, my head, and even my back hurts."

Mom felt his forehead. "Oh dear! Your forehead is very hot. That's it. You're staying home today." She left the room to call the school and Victor's doctor.

Victor pulled the covers over his head and quickly fell back asleep. He stayed in bed all day. Mom brought him his favorite books to read. She even told him he could play video games for an hour, but Victor was too tired to do much. He just felt like sleeping.

At lunch, Mom made chicken soup with lots of vegetables. "This is just what I needed," said Victor. He ate very slowly, but he finished it all. Then he read for a while. At last, Victor started feeling better.

Directions Read "Sick Day" together with your child. Have your child retell the most important events in order by telling the character's goals, how he tried to reach those goals, and whether or not he accomplished them.

Comprehension Lesson 11

Name _____

Read the article.

Bats and Echolocation

Some bats eat animals or fruit, but most bats eat insects. Bats hunt at night, early morning, and in late evening. This is when many insects are out. Bats have a system to help them get around and hunt in the dark.

Bats have great hearing. Many bats use sound as well as sight to move and find food at night. They give off short, high sounds through their noses and mouths. Then they listen for the echoes that bounce off of nearby objects. When a bat's sound hits something, such as an insect, the sound bounces back in the direction from which it came. Bats hear their sounds bounce back. Then they can tell the direction, distance, and size of things around them. They can also tell in what direction an object is moving. When they hunt, bats send out sounds faster and faster to track and catch food. This is known as echolocation.

Bats use echolocation to communicate with other bats. They also use it so they do not hit objects as they fly. Most importantly, bats use it to find and catch food.

Directions Have your child read "Bats and Echolocation" aloud. Have your child point out several main ideas in the article. Then have him or her summarize the article.

Read the story.

One Last Thing

Kim looked out the window. It was a hot, sunny day. She picked up her towel and swimsuit. "I am ready!" Kim told her mother.

Kim's mother had put some drinks and fruit in a bag. "Do we have all we need?" she asked.

"I think so," said Kim. They walked to the car. Kim's mother picked up two chairs and put them in the trunk.

"Oh, no!" said Kim. "I need one more thing." She ran back to the house. She came back with a small bottle.

"What's that?" asked Kim's mother. "It's my sunscreen," said Kim. "Yes," said Kim's mother, "we will need lots of that today!"

Directions Read "One Last Thing" together with your child. Ask, "What does this story remind you of in your life?" "Have you ever forgotten something?" and "What happened?"

Comprehension Lesson 12

Read the article.

Life in the Desert

Deserts are hot and dry. It is hot during the day. It is cold at night. There is little water in a desert. Rain might not fall for months in some places. Other places might not get rain for years.

Animals have learned how to live in the desert. Some animals come out only at night. Other animals live under the ground. This helps them stay cool. These animals also have ways to save water. Some animals, such as camels, can go a long time without water. Many desert animals get water from the things they eat.

Directions Before reading "Life in the Desert" with your child, ask, "What do you already know about the desert?" Then read the article. Ask, "What other articles or things in your own life does this article remind you of?" and "Why?"

Name _____

Read the article.

The Truth About Spiders

There are many kinds of spiders. All spiders have eight legs, and many have eight eyes. Spiders do not have ears. They can "hear" things because the tiny hairs on their legs vibrate if something near them makes a sound.

All spiders have two parts. One part is a head. The other part is called the abdomen. The abdomen is filled with light blue blood.

Spiders live for about one year. As they grow, they shed their skins and grow new ones. This can happen many times.

Spiders can live in many different places. Some live in dry places. Some live in wet places. They can live in hot and cold places. They can even live in water.

Many spiders make webs to live on. Other spiders do not make webs. Some of them like to live under the ground or in flowers.

Although many people fear spiders, most spiders cannot hurt people. You should also know many spiders eat insects that most people consider pests.

Directions Before reading "The Truth About Spiders" with your child, ask, "What do you already know about spiders?" Then read the article. Ask, "What other articles or experiences from your own life does this article remind you of?"

Read the story.

The Ant and the Dove

An ant went to the edge of a river to take a drink, but it was swept away by the fast-moving water. The ant was about to drown. He tried to swim to shore, but it was no use. He cried out for help. Just then, a dove sitting on a branch nearby saw him. The dove took a leaf and let it fall into the river near the ant. The ant was so happy! He climbed onto the leaf and floated to safety. The ant promised he wouldn't forget the dove's kindness.

Later, an animal came along and stood under the tree, hunting the dove. The ant saw the animal and rushed toward it. Then the ant crawled on the animal and stung it on its leg. The animal yelled in pain, which scared the dove away.

School + Home

Directions Have your child read aloud "The Ant and the Dove." Ask, "Have you read a story like this before?" and "What does this story remind you of in your own life?" Then ask, "Did you think the ant would help the dove?" Help your child identify how background knowledge helped him or her predict that the ant would help the dove.

Name _____

Read the article.

India's Taj Mahal

The Taj Mahal is one of the most well-known places in the whole world. In English, the name means "crown palace." Millions of visitors come from all over to see the white marble buildings, gardens, and pools.

An emperor started building the Taj Mahal in 1632. He built it to honor his wife. He and his wife had fallen deeply in love. They were married in 1612. Then she died in 1631 during the birth of their child. The emperor was very sad. He wanted to build something beautiful to honor his wife.

It is believed that the emperor had planned on building a black marble building across the river. This building would hold his own remains after he died. A bridge over the river would connect the two buildings. However, after a war, the emperor's son became the ruler. He put his father in prison. The black marble building was never built.

The Taj Mahal took 22 years to build. More than 20,000 people and 1,000 elephants helped build it. Its buildings, pools, and gardens stretch over 40 acres. Now people from all over the world visit this beautiful place each year.

Directions After reading "India's Taj Mahal" with your child, ask, "What does this article remind you of from your life or from what you have read or seen?" Then ask, "What type of writing is this?" Help your child realize that identifying the type of writing helps him or her better understand the text.

Comprehension Lesson 12

Name _____

Read the story.

The Blind Men and the Elephant

Each Sunday six blind men met in a garden. One day a loud sound interrupted them.

"Excuse me," said a boy. "My elephant is hot and tired. Do you mind if we rest here?" None of the blind men had ever met an elephant. "You may touch him if you like," said the boy.

The first man touched the rough skin on the elephant's leg. "An elephant is just like a tree!" he said.

The second man felt the elephant's long tusk. "No, an elephant is as hard and smooth as marble," he said.

The third man touched the elephant's ear, which flapped back and forth. "No," he said, "an elephant is just like a fan!"

The fourth man pushed the elephant, but the animal would not move. "An elephant is just like a wall."

The elephant brushed his trunk lightly across the fifth man's neck. "An elephant is like a large snake!" the man yelled.

The sixth man lifted the elephant's thin tail. "No, an elephant is like a piece of rope," he said.

The men argued.

"Shhh," said the boy. "You are all right. You are also all wrong. An elephant is very large, and you each touched only part of him. If you add together all those things, you'll know what an elephant is really like."

Directions Before reading "The Blind Men and the Elephant" with your child, ask, "What do you already know about elephants from life or from what you have read?" Then read the story together. Ask, "What type of writing is this?" and "How does knowing that help you better understand the text?"

Name _____

Read the story.

Socks

    Juan is excited because his family is big now. Juan just got a
new puppy named Socks. Socks is still very young. Juan is teaching
him how to be a good dog. Sometimes Juan catches Socks with
a shoe in his mouth. Socks likes to bite things into little pieces!
Most of the time, Socks is good. He sleeps next to Juan's bed. He
is learning how to take walks. Often Socks acts like Juan's shadow.
He follows Juan all over the house.

Directions Read "Socks" with your child. Before reading, have your child preview the passage and art and ask questions about what he or she wants to know. After reading, have your child ask and answer questions about *who* is in the story, *what* happens, and *why* it happens.

School + Home

Read the story.

Zebras at the Zoo

Last week, my parents took me to the zoo. I love going to the zoo! I like to see all the animals. I like the zebra the best. Zebras have black and white stripes. A zebra looks a little like a horse.

We got to the zoo. First, we saw the monkeys playing. Then we saw the elephants. I looked for the zebras. It was a hot day. The elephants blew water on each other to cool off. We kept walking. At last, I saw the sign for the zebras. They were playing and chasing each other in the grass.

Directions Read "Zebras at the Zoo" with your child. During reading, have your child pause to ask questions about anything he or she finds confusing. After reading, have your child ask and answer questions about *who* is in the story, *what* happens, and *where* and *when* it happens.

Name _____

Read the story.

Trip to Grandma's

Max and Jaime couldn't wait to go to Grandma's house. They were too excited to eat breakfast. They helped put the suitcases in the car. Then they got in their seats and buckled their seat belts. Dad got in the front seat to drive. They were on their way!

When they stopped for lunch, Dad ordered some sandwiches and fruit. Max and Jaime took a few bites of their sandwiches. They didn't eat any of the fruit. Dad said it would be a few more hours before they arrived at Grandma's house. The boys wanted to get back on the road.

When they finally got to Grandma's house, the boys were feeling tired. They had hardly eaten all day, and they didn't have much energy. Grandma decided to make a healthy snack for everyone.

Max and Jaime ate some granola and dried fruit. They felt a lot better now that they had more energy. The trip to Grandma's had been long and hot. But now they were with their favorite person of all—Grandma.

Directions Encourage your child to pause to ask and answer questions before, during, and after reading. Then have your child read "Trip to Grandma's" aloud. Discuss what happens in the story and how it happens. Encourage your child to ask clarifying questions, such as, "Why were the boys tired when they got to Grandma's house?"

Comprehension Lesson 13

Name _____

Read the story.

Look Both Ways

Johnny and his little brother Frank were walking to school. As they walked, they talked about the special visitor who was coming to school that day. Officer Jones was going to talk about street safety. Frank thought he already knew enough about street safety, but he was excited to meet a real police officer.

The boys came to a corner and were about to cross the street. Frank stepped off the curb. Just then, Johnny grabbed Frank's hand to pull him back. "You have to look both ways before crossing the street!" he scolded his brother. Frank realized that maybe he needed to learn more about street safety than he thought.

When they approached the school, Johnny and Frank saw the crossing guard. They waited at the curb. The crossing guard stopped the traffic. Before they crossed, Frank stopped Johnny. When Johnny gave him a puzzled look, Frank reminded him that he should look both ways before crossing the street!

Directions Have your child read "Look Both Ways" aloud. Encourage your child to ask questions about the meanings of unfamiliar words, such as *approached* or *puzzled*. Have him or her also ask and answer clarifying questions, such as, "Why does Frank stop Johnny even though the crossing guard allows them to cross?"

School + Home

Read the story.

First Day of School

It was the first day of school. Jim was worried and excited. He put all of his school supplies in his new backpack. He set his backpack by the front door so he would not forget it. Then his mother called out to him, "Hurry up!" She told him to get into the kitchen, grab his lunch, and jump in the car. They were running a little late.

Jim grabbed his lunch and carried it with him through the back door and into the garage. He got into the car and buckled his seat belt. Then his mother pulled out of the garage and headed toward school. A few blocks away, Jim realized he did not have his backpack.

Jim's mother dropped Jim off at school. He was worried because he did not have any of his school supplies. His mother told him to borrow some from his friends. Yet when she saw the look on Jim's face, she knew what she had to do. She went back to the house, picked up Jim's backpack, and dropped it off at school. When Jim got his backpack, he felt a little less worried and a lot more excited about his first day of school.

Directions Have your child read the first two paragraphs of "First Day of School." Then have your child pause to ask questions about what he or she has read so far. Before your child reads the final paragraph, ask, "What do you think will happen next?" After reading, have your child ask and answer any remaining questions.

Read the article.

Laura Ingalls Wilder

As a young girl, Laura Ingalls Wilder quickly became used to the struggles and adventures of pioneer life. Her father dreamed of going west to settle new land. He moved his wife and four daughters from state to state, crossing forests, plains, and the Mississippi River.

Moving often made it hard for Laura and her sisters to go to school. Still, Laura's family felt school was important. When she was older, Laura became a teacher.

She then met her husband, and the two were married. Their first years together were not easy. Their crops died, they had a lot of debt, they both became sick, and their young son died. They also had one daughter, Rose. Rose would later give Laura the courage to write about her own life.

Laura's daughter Rose had always loved hearing her mother's childhood stories. After Rose became a writer herself, she encouraged her mother to write down her stories. With Rose's help and inspiration, Laura began writing fiction. At the age of 65, Laura finished her first book, *Little House in the Big Woods*. It was about Laura's early life. She later published several other Little House books. Her books are still widely read today.

Directions Before reading, have your child preview the article and tell what he or she knows about Laura Ingalls Wilder and pioneer life. As your child reads, have him or her pause to ask questions and to make predictions. After reading, have him or her ask and answer any remaining questions.

Name _____

Read the article.

Getting a Puppy

Taking care of a puppy is hard work, but it can also be a lot of fun.

You will need to prepare your house. Find a place for your puppy to eat. Find a place for it to sleep too.

Your puppy will need to go out. Take it for lots of walks.

Your puppy will need to visit a vet. The vet gives shots. The vet helps your puppy get better when it gets sick. You can help your puppy, too. Brush it and keep it clean.

Your puppy also needs to play. You will have lots of fun with your puppy!

A vet is an animal doctor.

Directions Read "Getting a Puppy" with your child. Have your child read the title, look at the picture, and read the caption. Ask, "What do the title, illustration, and caption show that might be important?" Then ask, "What are some important ideas in this passage?"

Name _____

Read the story.

The Old Glove

Paul and Tom had ball practice together. Tom let Paul try out his glove. Paul slid his hand into the leather. It was old but very soft. The glove had been Tom's father's when he was a boy.

Tom was going on a trip the next week. "You can borrow my glove while I am gone," he said. Paul was excited.

Paul practiced with the glove every day. He caught every ball wearing that glove. Then one day he could not find the glove. He looked all over. At last, he asked his mother. She was getting ready for a yard sale.

"Do you mean this old thing?" she asked. "I was going to sell it in the sale."

It was Tom's glove! Paul pulled it out of the box. He found it just in time!

School + Home **Directions** Read "The Old Glove" with your child. Ask, "What ideas do you think are important?" Then ask, "What details are *not* important?" and "Why?"

Name _____

Read the story.

Lunch at Aunt Hilda's

Sam went to visit his Aunt Hilda. He had never met his aunt before. He saw a picture once. She looked really mean.

He walked up to the big, dark, and scary house. Aunt Hilda opened the door. She didn't smile as Sam walked in. She just pointed down the hallway and said, "Go eat lunch in the dining room."

Sam thought, "I bet it's broccoli. I hate broccoli!"

He went into the huge dining room. It was the size of a soccer field! His aunt put a tray in front of him. He saw that it was his favorite—pizza and ice cream! Aunt Hilda smiled and said, "Your mother told me these were your favorites."

He smiled back. Maybe Aunt Hilda wasn't so mean after all!

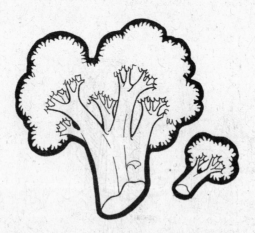

Directions Have your child read "Lunch at Aunt Hilda's" aloud. After each paragraph, ask, "What is the important idea in this paragraph?" Then ask, "What details support this idea?"

Comprehension Lesson 14

Read the article.

Sally Ride

Sally Ride was the first American woman to go into space. She went into space in June 1983. The second time she went into space was October 5 to October 13, 1984.

Sally Ride was born in California in 1951. She studied science in school. One day she saw an ad in a newspaper. The ad said the government was looking for people who wanted to join the space program and go into space. She answered the ad and was chosen for the space program in 1978.

On June 18, 1983, Ride went on her first mission into space on the shuttle *Challenger*. The mission lasted six days. During the mission, she worked with satellites and performed experiments. On her second mission in October 1983, Ride's childhood friend Kathryn Sullivan was also part of the crew.

After her work as an astronaut, Ride became a professor. Since then, she has started many programs to help young people get involved in science, math, and technology.

Directions Have your child read "Sally Ride" aloud. After each paragraph, ask, "What is the important idea in this paragraph?" Then ask, "What facts and details support this idea?"

Name _____

Read the article.

The Moon

The moon is an interesting place. It does not have any air. The moon is a cold and dusty place. Its surface has a lot of holes called *craters*. The craters were made by pieces of rock that crashed into the moon.

The moon also has seas, but they are not like the seas on Earth. The moon's seas do not have water. They are flat pieces of land.

The moon spins around, just like Earth does. We only see one side of the moon as it moves around Earth. You would have to go into space to see the other side of the moon. The moon moves around Earth. Its path is called an *orbit*. It takes 28 days for the moon to move all the way around Earth.

People have gone into space and walked on the moon. They collected rock and soil samples. They brought them back to Earth.

Some people think they can see the "man in the moon." No one lives on the moon. Light and dark parts of the moon just look a little like a face.

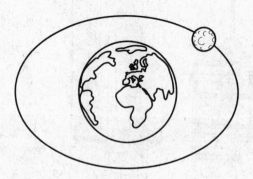

Directions Have your child read "The Moon" aloud. Ask, "What are the important ideas in the article?" Have your child list details and facts from the article that support each important idea. Then ask, "Why do you think the author wrote this article?"

Comprehension Lesson 14

Name _____

Read the article.

Sharks

Many people are afraid of sharks. They think of them as killers. However, they are interesting animals.

Sharks have lived on Earth for more than 400 million years. They swam in the oceans before the dinosaurs were born. The first sharks were much larger than the ones we see today. Other than that, they have changed very little over time.

Sharks have very strong teeth. Some have teeth that are strong enough to cut through steel. They use their teeth to bite their prey. Then they swallow the food whole. If they lose a tooth, one grows in right away. Some sharks have 3,000 teeth in their mouths.

Sharks are very good at finding food. They start hunting as soon as they are born. They eat meat. They use their senses of smell and hearing to find their prey. They can hear a sound as far as 700 feet away. When sharks hear another animal, they move close to it. Then they use their sense of smell to find it.

More than 350 kinds of sharks live in our oceans. They might seem dangerous, but they are interesting animals!

School + Home

Directions Have your child read "Sharks" aloud. Ask, "What are the important ideas in the article?" Have your child list details and facts from the article that support each important idea. Then ask, "Why do you think the author wrote this article?"

Name _____

Read the passage.
Draw a picture of a farm in the box.

At the Farm

I saw many animals when I went to the farm. There were cows in the barn. It was painted red and white. The cows in it were white and black. I milked a cow. The milk tasted thick and warm.

I saw horses out in a field. People were riding the horses. They raced across the wet grass. I could hear them pounding the ground as they ran.

The farm has chickens too. I helped the farmer pick up the eggs. I held a baby chicken. It was soft and yellow.

It was fun to see all the animals at the farm. I cannot wait to go back!

Directions Read "At the Farm" aloud to your child. Have your child picture the passage in his or her mind. Then read it a second time together. Have your child make a drawing in the box of what he or she visualized.

　　　　　　　　　　Comprehension Lesson 15

Name _____

Read the story.

Getting Ready

Ann takes out a small box. It has a picture of a car on it. She cuts a large piece of thin, blue paper. Ann tapes the paper around the box. Then she tapes a bow on top.

Ann takes out some blue balloons. She blows them up. Then she tapes them around the room. Without looking, Ann steps on one. It pops with a loud *bang!* She jumps.

Then Ann brings in the warm cake from the kitchen. She places it in the middle of the table. Soon the whole room smells like cake. Ann tastes the sweet frosting with her finger.

Now everything is ready for her son's birthday party!

Sight	Hearing	Smell	Touch	Taste

Directions First, read "Getting Ready" aloud to your child. Have your child picture the story in his or her mind. Then read it a second time together. Ask, "What did you picture in your mind as you read the story?" and "Which senses did the story make you think of?" Have your child jot responses in the chart.

Name _____

Read the story.

Young Paul Bunyan

People were excited when Paul Bunyan was born. He was so heavy that it took five giant storks to deliver him to his parents. He grew so fast that he had to wear his father's clothes while he was still a baby.

Paul's parents used a logging wagon as a baby carriage. The wheels squeaked and groaned under the weight. When Paul grew too big, his parents put him to sleep on a raft in the ocean. His rocking in his sleep caused big, crashing waves that sank ships.

On his first birthday, his father gave him a pet blue ox named Babe. Babe grew to be over 10 feet wide. Babe would eat 30 bales of hay for a snack, rusty wire and all. When he was thirsty, he emptied whole rivers with one drink. Paul and Babe were so large that the tracks they made while running all over the state of Minnesota filled up with rain and made the 10,000 lakes.

Comprehension Lesson 15

Read the first paragraph of the story. Then read the rest of the story.

The Chase

Bill walked up to the house. He noticed that the kitchen door was open. Inside, the house was a mess. He could hear his cat meowing as if she were afraid. "Oh, no!" thought Bill. Had someone broken in?

Then Bill saw muddy paw prints all over the floor. Some were small, and some were large. He thought he smelled a dog, but he didn't own a dog.

Bill walked into the next room. He saw pieces of newspaper all over the floor. There was gray fur all over the couch. He called for Sam, his gray cat. Then he saw a dirty bone under a chair. That was odd.

Just then Bill heard a whistle and a young boy's voice. "Rusty! Bad Dog! Come here now!"

Bill walked into the living room. "Hello?" he asked. "Who's there?" Then he saw Sam stuck on the top shelf of the bookcase. Rusty, the neighbor dog, was staring at him from the floor. Timmy, Rusty's owner, was pulling on his leash, but Rusty would not move.

Then Timmy saw Bill. "Bill! I'm so sorry! Rusty saw Sam in the yard, and he chased her inside your house!"

Bill slapped his forehead and shook his head. "At least it wasn't a burglar!" he thought.

Directions Read the first paragraph of "The Chase" and have your child visualize what is happening. Ask, "What did you picture in your mind?" Then read the rest of the story. Ask, "How did you change the picture in your mind?"

Read the story.

The Giant and the Villagers

A giant lived in a house on the side of a steep mountain. Every morning the giant woke up with the shining sun. He got out of bed and stood outside the door. He stretched his arms and stood very tall, so he blocked the sun to the valley below. This made the villagers cold and angry.

When the giant caught a cold, his every sneeze caused a terrible windstorm. Each sneeze was a loud howl that covered the villagers in dust. Some houses in the village even lost their roofs because of the wind from his sneezes. The villagers were unhappy.

One day the giant began to cry because he was reading such a sad book. Tears rolled down his face and caused a flood in the valley. The flood rotted the wood and houses started to smell. The villagers were soaking wet and upset.

The villagers had to do something.

First, they gave the giant an alarm clock, so he woke before the sun came up. Then the town cooks brought him tasty chicken soup, so his cold went away. The town's children read him a different book each day. Every book was a happy book. Finally both the giant and the villagers were happy.

Sight	Hearing	Smell	Touch	Taste

Directions Have your child read "The Giant and the Villagers" aloud. Ask, "What did you picture in your mind as you read the story?" Have your child find at least one descriptive detail in the story for each of the five senses (sight, hearing, smell, touch, taste) and write them in the chart.

Comprehension Lesson 15

Name _____

Read the article.

Make a Pine Cone Bird Feeder

Do you enjoy the songs of birds in your yard? Do you like to watch red robins, yellow finches, and gray doves feeding together near your picture window? Attract these and other birds with a simple bird feeder. You can make one yourself in no time!

First, find a large, dry, pine cone. Check that the pine cone is not damp and does not smell musty. Brush off any dirt or moss so that the scales of the pine cone are clean and smooth. Then tightly tie a piece of bright yarn around the top of it for the hanger.

Next, mix 2 tablespoons of crunchy peanut butter with 2 tablespoons of margarine. Spread the sticky mixture on the pine cone.

Then pour some bird seed on a plate and roll the pine cone in it. Sprinkle more seeds on the pine cone so that it is covered. Place the seed-covered pine cone in the freezer for about an hour or until it is hard.

Now you can hang the pine cone in a tree for birds to enjoy. Note that the sweet taste of the peanut butter may also attract squirrels. Be sure to hang your feeder in a spot where only birds can reach it.

Sight	Hearing	Smell	Touch	Taste

Directions Have your child read "Make a Pine Cone Bird Feeder" aloud. Ask, "What did you picture in your mind as you read the article?" and "How did visualizing help you picture what to do for each step of the process?" Then have your child find descriptive details for each sense and write them in the chart.

Name _____

Cause and Effect

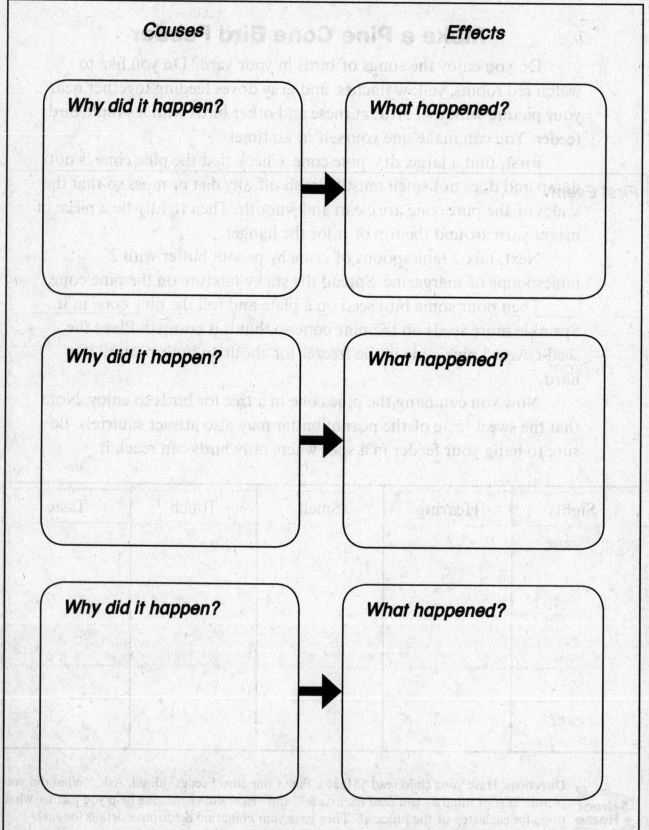

Causes   Effects

Why did it happen?   **What happened?**

Why did it happen?   **What happened?**

Why did it happen?   **What happened?**

                                                  Comprehension

Name _____

Events in a Story

Title

First Event

Next Event

Next Event

Last Event

Name _____

Five-Column Chart

Comprehension

Four-Column Chart

Main Idea

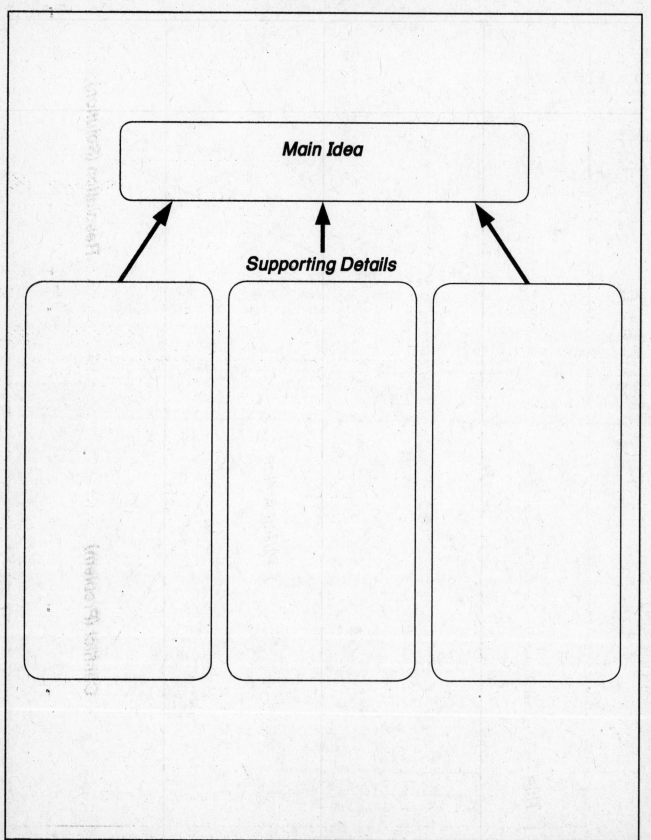

Main Idea

Supporting Details